Related Events to the Second Coming of the Christ

ARMAGEDDON

MESSIAH AND THE RESCUE OF ISRAEL

Volume 6

Michael W. Dewar

Copyright © 2023 by Michael W. Dewar
CORONATION OF THE CHRIST & THE MARRIAGE SUPPER OF THE LAMB
Related Events to the Second Coming of Jesus

ISBN: 979-8-9856973-4-6

Published by Dwelling Place Publishers
Brooklyn, New York 11236
United States of America
DPSCleansing.com

All rights reserved solely by the author. The author guarantees all contents are original and do not infringe upon the legal rights of any other person or work. No part of this book may be reproduced in any form without the permission of the author.

Unless otherwise indicated, Bible quotations are taken from The Holy Bible, New International Version(NIV). Copyright © 1973, 1978, 1984 by International Bible Society; The Holy Bible, King James Version(KJV); and The Holy Bible, New Living Translation(NLT). Copyright © 1996 by Tyndale House Publishers, Inc.

Dedicated
To my beloved niece Marjorie Dewar
And to my grandson Jordan. May good health
and the blessings of the Almighty be your always.

Armageddon, the war that ends all wars.

CONTENTS

Preface vii

Introduction 9

CHAPTER 1 13

Armageddon and Its Significance 13

CHAPTER 2 23

Armageddon and the Role of Israel 23

CHAPTER 3 41

The Rescue of Israel 41

CHAPTER 4 57

Israel's Indictment 57

CHAPTER 5 65

 The Judgment of Israel 65

CHAPTER 6 75

The Judgment of Nations 75

CHAPTER 7	87
The Salvation of Israel	87
End Notes	99
About the Author	101
Other Books By this Author	103

PREFACE

Welcome to Volume 6 in the series on *Related Events to the Second Coming of the Christ*. In Volume 5 Christ finally returns to earth as promised, and He returns in pageantry, glory, majesty, and might. But He comes in the posture of war because the controlling powers of the nations are no more welcoming of Him than they were at His first advent. But Israel as a nation is overjoyed for their deliverance but astonished to see that the One they rejected for so long is truly Israel's Messiah.

His *First Advent* was in peace and goodwill for all humankind, but King Herod sent out a unit of the Roman Legion to murder Him in the cradle. But He escaped that demise by crossing borders as a refugee into Egypt (Matt.2: 1-23).

Despite the prophetic evidence in the Hebrew Bible, and evidence of quality miracles never done before by anyone, He was not believed. Despite a ministry of good news concerning the Kingdom of God, good deeds done to countless lives, He was rejected by His own people, falsely accused by them, and handed over to the Romans to be executed. They hung Him high and stretched Him wide on a Roman cross on a hill called Calvary until He was dead.

But that ghastly event turned out to be the triumphant beginning of a new day of hope for humankind. That lowly life is still the drama of God's love and grace, not just the tragic end of an innocent life. Powerful people had Him killed, covered up the truth of His resurrection, and tried to destroy His followers. Despite all that, Yeshua has now returned to the same people, not to avenge Himself, but to rescue them from their own demise. That is what Armageddon is, a rescue mission; it is the Prince of glory depriving the prince of darkness his cherished prize of annihilating the State of Israel and its people.

Yeshua, the Christ, has returned to complete His mission of redemption, give hope and a future to the hopeless, forgiveness to the penitent, justice to the guilty, and vindication to the innocent. Armageddon is another page in the unfolding drama of redemption. But in this case, the force of war is used for peace.

The volumes in this series are designed to get your feet wet in the vast ocean of revelation knowledge that awaits you concerning the Kingdom of God and the future of humankind. I hope you will take the opportunity to explore this rich treasure house of knowledge far beyond these introductory volumes.

I want to say thanks to all who have provided some form of support to make this volume and the others in the series possible. Thanks to the members and friends of the New York Congregational Baptist Church (NYCBC) for their constant support and prayers.

INTRODUCTION
The War that Ends all Wars

If there is one word that sums up the *First Advent of the Christ* to earth, it is the word peace. The Lord Jesus was God incarnate, and He came to us in a very non-threatening manner, as a baby in a manger, as the Prince of Peace (John 1:1-5,14). At His birth the anthem of the angels was "peace on earth and good will to all people" (Luke 2:14).

Throughout His short life, Jesus wielded no weapon of war, lead no army, and advocated the overthrow of no leader, king, or government. He posed no threat to individuals or institutions, but others in their insecurities may have viewed Him as a threat.

His mission was to provide redemption, personal, and relational peace with God for all humankind. This He promised to do through the sacrifice of Himself (Rom.5: 1-5; Eph. 2:14-18).

To that end, Yeshua avoided war and violence to achieve His redemptive purpose. For the same reason, He avoided any Barabbas-type revolutionary gesture, such as being taken by force and crowned king, which would put Him in conflict with Caesar's government. But others who had such agendas were willing to frame Him when He refused to be used by them.

Jesus told Pilate, the Roman governor, that His kingdom was not of this world; if it were, his followers would fight to prevent Him from being arrested. Peter did come to His defense with a sword, but Jesus commanded him to put it away (Matt.26:52).

If He needed defense, He could have called "twelve legions of angels" to His defense (v.53). A Roman Legion at the time was six thousand soldiers. Jesus did not call angels to His defense because His mission was not to start a bloody revolutionary war, but to bring peace on earth for all humankind (Luke 1: 10-14).

Yeshua lived and taught peace as a duty of His followers, "Blessed are the peacemakers for they shall be called children of God" (Matt.5:9). Despite His lofty mission of redemption and peace for all humankind, His life ended violently on Roman gallows. At His command, His followers continued the mission of redemption and peace, but their lives ended violently too. Paul was beheaded, Peter was crucified upside down, others were tortured by various means, some throne to the lions.

Since the fall of man in the Paradise Garden, earth has been a rogue Planet under the influence of a rogue angel named, Lucifer or Satan. He is the rival Prince of darkness, bent on using war to dethrone the *Prince of Glory*, to prevent Him from returning to the earth to reign.

INTRODUCTION

The prince of darkness has been itching for a showdown because he refused to accept the defeat verdict of the cross where the *Seed of the Woman* crushed his head (Gen.3: 15). Satan's rebellion must be dealt with more definitively at the time and place of God's choosing. That showdown is called, Armageddon, and it is the world at war one last time.

The word Armageddon whether used theologically, or by the Hollywood entertainment industry, tends to strike fear in the hearts of people; it shouts to us that medga evil is coming, evil that will drastically alter one's way of life, if not extinguish life completely. All that and more is true of biblical Armageddon; it is already casting its long shaddow across the earth. Its approach is evident from the rumbling hoves of the four horsemen of the apocalypse in th distance, but advancing fast toward us.

In other words, the Armageddon spoken of in this book is the not the fictionalized version advanced by Hollywood, but the real thing, the m*ega-war* spoken of in the apostle John's apocalypse (Rev.16:16). It is the final showdown between good and evil. It is the ultimate cosmic conflict that brings the collective armed forces of earth into combat with God almighty and His Christ. It is over who has legitimate ownership of the earth and who controls the destiny of humankind. It is the final World War that ends all wars!

This volume looks at Armageddon, not so much as a war between the mighty of earth and the Almighty of heaven, which would be a war of no contest. But more of God rescuing Israel, His covenant people, from annihiliation at the hands of mighty Gentiles powers under the direction of the Antichrist.

The author paints in broad strokes; he does not track down unnecessary details. But, first defines the proper meaning of the word Armageddon and its significance. Second, this global War is looked at in the context of other events such as the Great Tribulation, the second advent of the Christ, the role of Israel, and the decisive outcome of this mega-military conflict.

Additionally, several sub-themes are briefly included, such as the antichrist, the 144,000 Israelites sealed (Rev.7:1-8), the woman and the red dragon (Rev.12:1-12), the judgment of Israel (Rev.20: 4-5), and the judgment of gentile nations (Matt.25:31-46), to name a few.

The whole world should know that the lead story at the *Second Advent of the Christ* will not be cerenading angels to shepherds on a Judean hill in Palestine, or wisemen tracking a guiding star to a manger in Bethlehem. But a war horse, a milk white stallion and its rider decending from the Eastern sky with an army of saints and angels and advancing toward Jerusalem to the Ground Zero of mega war (Rev.19:11-21). One word sums it up, Armageddon! We already know it is no ordinary war, but why is it called Armageddon (Rev.16:16)?

We will explore these and other questions in this volume without getting lost with overwhelming details. Every human being will be on one side or the other of this conflict, by choice or by default. It is the hope of this author that you will be a soldier on the side of the commander who is Jesus Christ. This you must do by choice, not by default. The side you are already on is likely the side you will remain, but you can change.

CHAPTER 1
ARMAGEDDON
AND ITS SIGNIFICANCE

What Is Armageddon, and why is its significant? People commonly use the word today to mean a horrific event of significant magnitude, a mega conflict or disaster that could end life on earth as we know it. The word Armageddon springs from the biblical word *Megiddo* with its own unique meaning. It signifies the final World War that ends all wars.

The word comes down to us from Greek (*Armageddon*) and Hebrew (*har M^egiddo*) which means "Hill or City of Megiddo," or a high place overlooking the valley of Megiddo, an ancient military site where several national leaders of antiquity won great victories or met their demise in war.[1]

Megiddo is the place Barak, a prominent judge of Israel, fought and won a great victory over the Canaanites, and Gideon won over the Midianites (Judges 4:14-23, 7: 1-25). King Saul, the first king of Israel, and his son Jonathan met their demise in war at Megiddo on the same day (1Sam.31: 8). Megiddo is also the place King Josiah was struck down in war (2 Kings 23: 29-30; 2 Chron.35: 22-24).[2] All these wars had the markings of divine intervention or judgment, which signal to us that the final mega war will be of the same character.

Megiddo then is the place from which Armageddon takes its name; it is often used synonymous to something horrible, mega, and final in its destructive force. But even though Megiddo is a real place, and the coming mega war is real—Armageddon is often used symbolically, referring to the final war between personified good and evil (Rev.16:16).[3]

It will be fought in the Middle East because the nation of Israel will be the primary reason for this war; the collective Gentile powers will seek to annihilate her. While the war is certain, we cannot dogmatically assert that it will be fought in the exact location as the ancient battles referred to here.

But due to its magnitude, horrific nature, and finality, this coming War is referred to as Armageddon. World War I and II combined with the two Gulf wars will fade into insignificance to the coming Armageddon war. It is Satan with his human proxies who have finally gotten full control of unregenerate humankind, world government, world financial resources, world institutions of worship, and the world's collective nuclear arsenal (Rev.13). Israel will be in the crosshairs of this war, the lamb among ravenous gentile wolves who are bent on her destruction.

Armageddon's Uniqueness

The skeptics and some critical theists have asked, why now? In other words, if Armageddon is indeed the final mega war, the showdown between good and evil, why did it take God that long to deal with personified evil? Has that delay made Satan too big for his proverbial *britches*, that he can now vigorously lay claim to the earth that he did not create? These questions give the impression that God is to be blamed for being passive against Satan and evil too along. Such charge demands a response.

First, the charge exposes great ignorance of God and how He works. The God of the Bible has been actively fighting evil from Satan's insurrection in heaven, a rebellion that got him and his cohorts thrown out of heaven. The Bible tells us that "war broke out in heaven. Michael and his angels fought against the dragon, and the dragon and his angels fought back. But he was not strong enough, and they lost their place in heaven." Satan and his angels were expelled (Rev.12:7-9). The move to expel Satan and his cohorts, can hardly be considered passive on God's part.

Second, when Satan inspired a rebellion in the human family in the Paradise Garden, all the actors in that rebellion, including Adam and his wife, had to face the consequences. They were tried and expelled from their paradise home, and the serpent that beguiled the woman also face the judgment of God (Gen.3:1-24). God cannot be charged for being passive toward evil in this case either. The rebellion against Him was put down.

Neither can God be charged for being passive toward the murderer Cain who took his brother's life without penitence. God held him accountable, tried and sentenced him for his crime (4:1-15). God's aversion to wickedness and His commitment to justice are well demonstrated in the flood of Noah's generation, the Babel Tower fiasco, and the demise of Sodom and Gomorrah (Gen.6:5-8,7:12-23;11:1-9,19:23-29). The exercise and restraint of God's judgment is evident in all these cases.

Third, the cross of Christ is God's remedy for dealing with the very root of evil, sin in the human heart. To effectively deal with Satan, the spiritual disease of sin that has infected the human family has to be dealt with first at the roots. Jeremiah reminds us that the inner sanctum of man, "the heart, is deceitful above all things, and desperately wicked" (Jer.17:9 KJV).

For these reasons, God became incarnate in the person of Jesus Christ, that *through death and resurrection* He might provide eternal salvation for the human family and *destroy Satan who once holds the power of death* (Heb.2:14).

Fallen humans consider God's method of the cross of Jesus Christ as the remedy to the sin problem as God's "foolishness and weakness," but the cross turns out to be "the wisdom and power of God" (1Cor.1:25, 2:7-8; Rom.1:16-17). Through the cross, God dealt with three major problems in one blow: the sin problem, the Satan problem, and the problem of death.

With reference to sin, its price was fully paid on the cross, thus giving every human being who want it, redemption, and forgiveness. With respect to Satan, the cross nullifies his power by crushing his head, thus, he is greatly restrained on a short leash. With reference to death, through His resurrection, Jesus conquered it for the human family.

Because of these three victories, the Word of God speaks confidently to the redeemed as follows: 1)*Concerning death*: "Knowing that Christ being raised from the dead dies no more;

death has no more dominion over Him" (Rom.6: 9 KJV). 2) *Concerning sin*: "For sin shall not have dominion over you for you are not under the law, but under grace" (Rom.6:14). 3) *Concerning Satan*: "Submit yourselves therefore to God. Resist the devil and he will flee from you" (Jas. 5:7).

Fourth, because God is almighty and omnipotent, He could have destroyed Satan from the time of his first rebellion, but that would not have fully dealt with the sin question or serve God's purpose. Satan serves a purpose in the economy of God. This is hard for some people to understand because they do not understand the sovereignty of God. The simple definition of sovereignty is that God is Almighty and omniscient, everything is under His control; everything serves His purpose.[4]

Yet, God hates sin and evil, and will bring judgment against them and will rid the creation of them in His time. In fact, God has been bringing judgment against sin and evil since Lucifer's rebellion and will eventually eradicate both from His creation in His own time. Until such time, evil serves the purpose of God. Some will ask, how can this be? We cannot exhaustively discuss this question in this work but will shed some light on it.

Perhaps, an illustration can help to explain it. It is like this— Joseph's eleven brothers conspired to murder him because they were jealousy of him. The murder plot failed because God would not allow it. So, to get rid of Joseph, the brothers sold him into slavery instead of killing him (Gen.37: 5-11, 19-28, 39: 1-6). And for them out of sight meant out of mind.

They brought home Joseph's bloody coat of many colors that they soaked in animal's blood, to make their concocted story more convincing. They told their parents that some ravenous beast devoured their son. Their parents believed the lie for over twenty years for it was so convincingly told. But they did not know that God was using their evil deeds to fast-tracking Joseph to the pinnacle of executive power as Prime minister of Egypt. God placed Joseph in a position of power to save many lives from death by starvation due to famine, including the lives of his cruel and wicked brothers.

When their wicked scheme was exposed after twenty years, Joseph was able to say to his brothers, "You intended to harm me, but God intended it for good to accomplish what is now being done, the saving of many lives" (Gen. 50:15-21).

Here is the lesson to learn—those who do evil will suffer the consequences, but God turns around some evil to His glory and to do much good over a short or long period of time. Joseph's brothers thought they got away with their wicked deeds, but they did not! God new their wicked heart in advance of their action and planned the outcome for His glory.

Why did God wait that long to expose their wickedness of Joseph's brothers? The answer is simple, God has a purpose in everything He does. So even the evils that Satan does through people, serve the purpose of God. But Satan does not know that because he is limited. He does not know all things; omniscience is an attribute of God alone. So, in a strange way, Satan serves God's purpose. Jesus defeated Satan on Calvary, but Satan mistakenly thought, he was the one who defeated Jesus Christ. The resurrection proved Satan wrong.

Fifth, Satan's rebellion (sin) is a judicial matter. The kingdom of God is a kingdom of laws, righteousness, truth, and justice. God has a specific time frame that He will judge the world in righteousness and justice through Jesus Christ (Acts 17:31). Everyone will get his or her due at the appointed time. Both angels and humans that join with Satan must be dealt with judicially because God is just in all His dealings.

There are angels that are so bad, they are currently kept in chains under darkness for the day of judgment (2 Peter 2:4; Jude 6). A group of demons feared Jesus was going to send them to hell before the appointed time cried out, have you come to torment us before the time? They pleaded that Jesus send them to inhabit pigs for the time being (Matt.8: 28-34).

The demons knew they will face judgment at an appointed time and will be sent to hell. But they did not want to go there before the time; they wanted due process. They know God is just and their case will be handled justly. Satan is already judged but not yet sentenced. His followers are not yet judged. Satan will be taken into custody at the *Second Advent* of the Christ (Rev.20:1-3). His followers of men and angels will be judge at the second advent and at the final judgment and will be thrown into hell with Satan (Matt.25:31-46; Rev.20:11-15). (See Vol. 9).

Sixth, to put it bluntly, Satan is restrained throughout the Church age, so that the message of salvation can be preached to all nations, giving humankind the opportunity for salvation (John 3:16). Humans are free moral agent and are free to exercise their choice to serve of God or not. Any inclination that a person want to serve God—God provides help to properly choose.

God is not compelling anyone to serve Him. The choice is ours to make; but choice comes with rewards or consequences. When the Church age has ended, the day of salvation for the gentiles will just about closed, but not completely closed. God will remove the restraint from Satan and all hell will break loose during the Great Tribulation; that will make it extremely difficult to be saved. The best time to be saved is now, because you are not likely to get your head cut off or get shot for doing so, especially in Western nations.

Satan's Restraint Removed

What is the restraint on Satan now? The short answer is the Church and the Holy Spirit. The Holy Spirit resides in the Church; that is, in the people of God, not church buildings. The Holy Spirit came on the Day of Pentecost to indwell the people of God and empower them to evangelize the world with the gospel, making disciples of all nations (Matt.28:19-20; Acts 1:8, 2:1-4).

The Day of Pentecost is considered the birthday of the Church. Since that day, the Church serves as salt and light in the world, restraining Satan and evil from becoming dominant. But this restraint will be removed when the Church is raptured to heaven (1 Thess.4:16-18; 2 Thess. 2:1-12). Since the Holy Spirit resides in the Church, His work ends as we now know it when the Church is gone (see Volume 1 *The Rapture*).

With the restraint on Satan and evil gone, all hell will break loose upon the earth. Through his human proxies, the Antichrist, and the False prophet (the two Beasts of Revelation 13), Satan now takes charge of world government, the global economic and monetary systems, the collective nuclear arsenal of earth, and all institutions of worship. The whole world is commanded to worship Satan; this will continue for seven years. The Bible calls this period, *The Great Tribulation* (see Volume 3).

Armageddon takes place at the end of the seven years of *Great Tribulation* when Christ returns to the earth with the Church that was previously raptured to heaven. He comes to take back His earth from Satan by putting down all oppositions to His authority. This come back is what is called, The Second Coming of the Christ or the Second Advent.

The Armageddon war is between the prince of darkness (Satan) who claims to be the god of this world and the Prince of Glory (Jesus Christ) who is the Creator and true owner of the earth (Psalm 24:1). All this makes Armageddon unique above all wars waged on Planet earth. Because Satan is a spirit being, he needs human actors who can provide him bodies to work through. The Antichrist and the False prophet are Satan's chief human cohorts heading his operation (Rev.13:1-3,11-12).

Satan models his kingdom off the Kingdom of God, and that is expected because Satan is not a creator; he is an imitator. As such, he structures his enterprise according to the one he knows and formerly worked for. But operates his kingdom to counter the purpose of God. Satan imitates God the Father, so you don't see him, but he is there behind the scenes. Of course, he does not imitate God's moral attributes, that would make him a good fellow. Yet, Satan will do good if it serves his evil purpose.

The Antichrist whom people will see, imitates God the Son who has a visible body (Rev.13:1-3). Jesus was visible to us until He returns to heaven, and He will be visible upon His return to earth (Acts 1: 9-11; 1Thess.4:16-18).

The False prophet imitates God, the Holy Spirit. The False prophet has the power to perform great miracles, even call down fire from heaven to deceive people (Rev.13:11-18). He will be a trusted religious leader with global reach, like an evil pope. These three characters: Satan, the Antichrist, and the False prophet are called by Bible scholars, the unholy trinity.

The job of the unholy trinity is to preemptively setup Satan's kingdom over the earth with humans, whom they will force to worship Satan. That is the way Satan seeks to legitimize himself as the god of this world—by commanding his followers to worship him (Rev.13:4-8, 11-15). Worship is what Satan has always wanted, but unlike God, he has no standard for worship. He accepts worship however it comes. He will bribe people to worship him as he attempted to do with Jesus (Matt.4:8-11).

Why Satan wants the inhabitants of the earth to worship him? He is trying to prevent Jesus from returning to earth to reign with and through two covenant communities: the Church and Israel. Satan hates these two communities and has sought to destroy them throughout all of history (Rev.12:1-17).

Jesus upon His return will reign over the earth as KING of Kings and LORD of Lords from Jerusalem by sitting on the throne of David in Israel (Isa.9:6-7). Satan's agenda is to destroy Israel before Jesus gets here, so there is no nation to rule over. It is for that reason Satan and his cohorts with the collective military might of earth are gathered to annihilate State of Israel.

This is something Satan wanted to do all along, kill all the Jews before they gain momentum to form a Jewish State. That was Satan's agenda behind, anti-Semitism, the holocaust, and the hate many nations have directed toward the Jews over the centuries. Armageddon is Satan's last chance to achieve his goal.

CHAPTER 2
ARMAGEDDON
AND THE ROLE OF ISRAEL

The little nation of Israel plays a pivotal role in God's redemption plan for humankind. The foundation knowledge that we have of God, the creation of the natural world, the creation of man, his values, worth, and man's responsibility to God and neighbor all came down to us from the Hebrew people.

Israel also gave us the concept of monotheism (one God) when the ancient world believed in polytheism (many gods) or pantheism (everything is God). Western jurisprudence, and the history of redemption are all traceable to the Hebrew Bible.

The impact the Jewish-Christian ways of life made on the world is well documented and cannot be denied. The Hebrews are God's covenant people, traceable to Father Abraham. When God called Abraham and his wife Sarah, He had three things on His mind: nation building, global blessings, and redemption of the human family. These three things are capsulated in the following unconditional covenant with Abraham:

> I will make you a great nation, and I will bless you; I will make your name great, and you will be a blessing. I will bless those who bless you, and whoever curses you I will curse; and all peoples on the earth will be blessed through you. (Gen.12 1-3)

The preceding quote is God's mission statement, His core reason or purpose for calling the man Abraham to build a great nation, through whom He would bless all nations or peoples upon the earth. The promised blessing is two-fold: material and spiritual. Israel was raised up by God to be the conduit for the knowledge and blessing of God to entire human family.

One should not overlook God's commitment to Abraham's protection in the statement, "whoever curses you, I will curse," nor should the incentive to bless Abraham be overlooked, "I will bless those who bless you." The warning and the incentive are applicable on both the micro and macro levels.

In other words, it applies to the individual, to groups, as well as nations. Any individual, group or nation that blesses Israel will be blessed, and the same is true for those who curse Israel. God does not speak idle words or make suggestions. His words are executive orders to be followed (Isa.55:8-11).

Israel's Breach of Covenant

How would God bless the whole world through Israel? The blessing would come through the revelation knowledge that God would give of Himself through Moses and the Prophets, and the contribution Jews would make to the world through law, education, economics, medicine, and so on.

Have you checked lately how many Nobel Prize have been won by Jews?[1] Their contribution to the world is enormous, given their small percentage. Jews "represent less than 0.20% of the world's population but they represent 22% of all Nobel Laureates (208 out of 930)."[2] That alone should cause anyone to pause. Their contribution to civilization is enormous!

But the greater blessing for which God raised up Israel is spiritual. God intended to bring redemption and salvation from sin through His Son Yeshua, Israel's Messiah, to the entire world. Yeshua (Jesus) the Messiah (Christ) would come through the linage of King David to redeem Israel and the world. Israel would be the first to receive the Messiah, salvation from sin, and then offer the good news of the gospel to the rest of the world.

But on the spiritual side, Israel failed miserably. In fact, they began failing long before the Messiah arrived. After the death of Moses, it was Joshua given the charge to settle the Israelites in the promise land (Jos.1:1-11). Joshua successfully settled them into the Promised Land (Jos.23:1-16). But after the death of Joshua, they fell into idolatry. They went whoring after other gods in violation of the covenant given to them by God. The book of Judges records the facts of their whoring after other gods. Why the word whoring? The book of Hosea illustrates that the relationship between God and Israel was like a marriage.

Abraham, the father of the nation was a man of faith, he believed God and it was counted unto him for righteousness. The Lawgiver Moses tied the blessings of the covenant to faith and obedience (Deut.28:1-68). In total, the blessings and curses of the covenant cover 68 verses in the English Bible: 14 verses of blessings and 54 verses of curses. Israel said, yes to God, they would exercise faith and obedience in keeping the covenant (Exod.24:1-8, 34:10-35; Deut.6:1-25).

But Israel did not follow through as promised, so the curses of the covenant were released. Their disobedience caused them to be subjugated to and mistreated by other nations, even taken into exile to Assyria and Babylon, and trampled upon by other nations including Rome, and Nazi Germany in modern times.

But Israel's most catastrophic failure was their rejection of their Messiah, Yeshua (Jesus). They rejected Him and rallied the Roman authorities to put Him to death, even though they knew He was innocent of the charges they brought against Him. They rejected God's plan of salvation and forfeited the mission God had assigned them to bless the rest of the world.

God temporarily set them aside and formed a new body called, the Church. The Church is assigned the task of carrying out the work of evangelization; that is, to bring the good news of the gospel and salvation to the rest of the world (Matt.28:18-20; Mark 16:14-16; Acts 1:8). The apostles and the Early Church did their share as well as the Medieval Church. Great Britain and the United States have been greatly instrumental bringing the knowledge and light of the gospel to the world in the 19th and 20th centuries. The English Bible brought the light of the gospel to the Western world and beyond.

Because of Israel's lack of faith and obedience to the covenant and their rejection of the Messiah, Jesus Christ, they were driven off their covenant land and scattered to the ends of the earth (except for an *indigenous minority*). In 70 AD the Romans drove the final nail into Judaism's coffin as it existed during the time of Christ.

Jerusalem was besieged by the Roman army, the Jewish temple destroyed, thousands of Jews killed, thousands taken prisoners of war, the priesthood demolished, sacrifices ended, the Ark of the Covenant disappeared; Judaism ceased to be. The destruction of the temple fulfilled Jesus' Mount of Olives prediction on this matter (Matt.24:1-2).[3]

From 70 AD Israel remained a scattered people among the nations until the formation of the modern State of Israel in 1948. The process of regathering is still going on in 2023. Since 70 AD Judaism has not returned to what it used to be in the time of Jesus, that is, first century Judaism. Why is that so?

There is no temple, no sacrifice, no priesthood, no Ark of the Covenant, and no shekinah glory of God. The temple was most critical to Biblical Judaism; without it, you can't have the other missing pieces. Despite these missing fundamentals, however, Judaism has reconstituted itself but without its former glory.[4] The glory has departed, and Israel will remain in this state of Ichabod for the duration of her state of unbelief.

Nonetheless, through hard work, Jews prospered among the nations they were scattered, but the world has not been a kind place for them. Just about everywhere they went, Satan sought to destroy them. In their attempt to exterminate the Jews, Hitler's Germany slaughtered over six million of them.

We may sum up this section by saying that Israel's breach of covenant resulted in their expulsion from their covenant land. But God is faithful and will bring them back out of all the nations they have been scattered. God has not cast away His people.

The Regathering of Israel

Despite Israel's lack of faith and obedience to the covenant, their rejection of the Messiah, and they been driven off their covenant land, God has not cast away His people (Rom.10:1-6). The apostle Paul who himself was an Israelite, asserts that "blindness happened in part to the Israel until the fullness of the Gentiles [is brought into the kingdom of God]," then "all Israel will be saved" (Rom.11:25-26).

In other words, the Gentiles benefit from Israel's rejection because they became the primary beneficiaries of salvation. The apostle John writes that Jesus came to His own people, but they did not receive Him. But those that receive Him in faith are given the right to become children of God (John 1:11-12).

Israel's unbelief and rejection of Jesus Christ their Messiah, resulted in their expulsion from their covenant land, but not the cancellation or termination of ownership. The ownership clause of the covenant is unconditional. Otherwise, God would not have promised to regather His people out from among the nations He scattered them, and bring them back to their covenant land, and they will never be uprooted again (Deut.30:1-10; Ezek.36:24-30; 37:1-28). Israel's ownership of the land is permanent!

The modern rebirth of the State of Israel is nothing short of miraculous; it is the God of Abraham, Isaac and Jacob fulfilling His covenant promise to His people made long ago. This reality inspired Netanyahu, the longest serving Prime Minister of Israel to date to write: "The reemergence of the Jews as a sovereign nation is an unprecedented event in the history of mankind."[5]

Jesus speaking about His return and the end of the age, calls our attention to the fig tree (a symbol of the nation of Israel): "Now learn a lesson from the fig tree: As soon as its twigs get tender and its leaves come out, you know the summer is near. Even so, when you see these things, you know that it is near, right at the door" (Matt.24:32-33).

Students of prophecy agree that the rebirth of the State of Israel in these last days is the blooming of the proverbial fig tree; it signals the Lord's return is near, even at the door. Because a Jewish State must be in place for Jesus to rule over when He returns, according to prophetic writings (Isa.9:6-7; Jer.31:10).

The regathering of the Jewish people to Palestine to form the modern State of Israel, did not just happen or happen in a vacuum or overnight; it was decades in the making. In fact, the fig tree was not even a tree after AD 70 to begin with; it was a stump in the ground, but not a dead stump by any means.

The prophet Isaiah prophesied, "A shoot will come up from the stump of Jess; from his roots a Branch will bear fruit" (Isa.11:1,10; Rom.15:12). This stump began to bud again in the form of a movement to be later called, Zionism.

What is Zionism? Zionism is the collective will and longing in the hearts of Jewish people everywhere, to have their own homeland in Palestine; with hard work, this passion galvanized into a movement, called Zionism. It has taken a long process of Zionists' work coupled with people of good will, working hard over decades to bring about the modern State of Israel. Yes, God was and is involved, but faith without works is dead, the apostle James reminds us (Jas.2:4-26).

Fundamental to the realization of the modern Jewish State is the work of Theodor Herzl, the founder of Zionism. Herzl was a Hungarian Jew, born in Budapest 1860. But did much of his work in Vienna as a journalist. He was a man with the farsighted vision who advanced the idea that if the Jew was going to survive as a people, they must have their own homeland and the right to self-determination. He wrote and published a pamphlet in 1896 with the title, "The Jewish State" in which he proposed the answer to the Jewish question.[7]

Though the vision of a modern Jewish State in Palestine gained traction, sprouted wings, and flew with Herzl's burning passion; there were Jews before and after him with like vision.

In the 1880s before Herzl, a Jewish movement sprang up in Russia under the direction of "M.L. Lillienblum and Leo Pinkser" which inspired the building of Jewish settlements in Palestine.[8] After Herzl's short life, Jews and non-Jews from many nations rose to support the Zionist movement including Christians.

It is amazing how God has worked to bring about the fulfillment of His word at the turn of the 20th Century to regather His people to their covenant land. Several important events converged to bring about the reality of the modern Jewish State of which we cannot name all in this small volume, but four.

First, the work of Chaim Weizmann, "a Russian Jew who immigrated to England in 1904." He was a master chemist and a leader in the Zionist movement." During World War I, the British government sought Weizmann's help because their soldiers were using gunpowder made of cordite which not only had adverse effects on the soldiers, but it also produced smoke that would reveal their location to the enemy. Weizmann went to work and quickly developed a biochemical process for producing synthetic acetone to resolve the gunpowder problem which greatly contributed to the British and allies' victory.[9]

Second, as a Zionist leader pushing for a homeland in Palestine for the Jews, Great Britain remembered Weizmann's contribution, and "officially issued the Balfour Declaration of 1917, which declared: "His Majesty's Government views with favor the establishment in Palestine of a national home for the Jewish people and will use their best endeavors to facilitate the achievement of this object...."[10]

Third, the next influential event that brought Jews scattered among the nations back to Palestine is the liberation of Jewish prisoners from Nazi concentration camps such as Auschwitz, Dachau, and others. With the collapse of Germany at the end of World War II, the whole world was shock and horrified of the cruelty, the barbarism, the butchery of the Nazi regime against Jewish people. "This generated sympathy that drew Jewish wealth from around the world and enabled the relocation of more than a million displaced Jews to Palestine."[11]

Fourth, on the memorable day of May 14, 1948, the United Nations officially recognized the State of Israel with President Harry Truman of the United States casting the deciding vote. All this add up to the fulfillment of 2500 year-old prophecy recorded in the Bible. Indeed, God's word will not return to Him void but will accomplish its assigned purpose (Isa.55: 8-11).

It should be noted that the regathering of Israel to their homeland is an ongoing process in the 21st Century and will not be completed until the *Second Advent of the Christ*. God is also preparing Jews spiritually to receive Yeshua as their Messiah when He comes back. Frankly, only those who are spiritually changed will inherit the fulfillment of the covenant. Jesus is not going to draft unbelieving Israelites to reign with Him no more than He will draft unbelieving Gentiles. Notwithstanding, Paul speaks prophetically that all Israel will be saved (Rom.11:25-27).

Israel's In Satan's Crosshairs

Satan has always hated Israel and its people for at least three reasons: 1) they are God's covenant people, 2) the Messiah came through that nation, and 3) the Messiah will return to sit upon the throne King David's and rule over the world from Jerusalem (Isa.9: 6-7). Satan wants to preemptively move to destroy the Jews and occupy Jerusalem, thinking that will stop Jesus from coming to reign. Satan's hate is also directed at the Church which evolves out of Israel and is attached to Jesus.

Satan's hate for these two institutions (i.e., Israel and the Church) is clearly documented in the Bible and on the pages of secular history. Great nations have enslaved Israel and have done much to destroy her. Some of these nations have been reduced to second rate powers in the world, while others are relegated to trash heap of history.

Here are a few: Egypt, Assyria, Babylon, Persia (modern day Iraq & Iran), Rome, Spain, and Hitler's Germany. They have tried to destroy the Jewish people, but Israel is still around and doing well. Rome tried to destroy the Church and failed. But Satan is not through; his most audacious plan of attack is coming; the Bible calls it, Armageddon (Rev.16:12-16).

Satan's hate for Israel and the Church is descriptively laid out in the following scripture:

> A great sign appeared in heaven: a woman clothed with the sun, with the moon under her feet and a crown of twelve stars on her head. She was pregnant and cried out in pain as she was about to give birth.
>
> Then another sign appeared in heaven: an enormous red dragon with seven heads and ten horns and seven crowns on its head. Its tail swept a third of the stars out of the sky and flung them to the earth. The dragon stood in front of the woman who was about to give birth, so that it might devour her child the moment he was born.
>
> She gave birth to a son, a male child, who will rule all the nations with an iron scepter. And her child was snatched up to God and to his throne. The woman fled into the wilderness to a place prepared for her by God, where she might be taken care of for 1,260 days. (Rev.12:1-6)

The woman in the text is not the Virgin Mary as some suggest but Israel to which Mary belongs. The red dragon is Satan. The seven heads and ten horns represent a coalition of nations and leaders that form the one-world government under the Antichrist. The male child of the woman is Jesus Christ. Israel gave the world Jesus Christ; from birth, Satan tried to kill Jesus. King Herod massacred the children of Bethlehem in that effort (Matt.2:16-18). The child caught up to heaven speaks of the ascension of Jesus (Acts 1:9-11).

The seven headed-beast with ten horns and crowns appears several times in the book of revelation, as the antichrist and false prophet (Rev.13:1-10), as the scarlet color, harlot riding beast which represents false religion (Rev.17:3-7). Again, the beast is the one-world government and apostate religion headed up by Satan, but the human faces are the Antichrist and the False prophet, the twin beast of Revelation 13.

Now, notice how furious the dragon became against the woman (Israel) who produced the male child (Jesus Christ):

> When the dragon saw that he has been hurled to the earth, he pursued the woman who had given birth to the male child. The woman was given two wings of a great eagle, so that she might fly to the place prepared for her in the wilderness, where she should be taken care of for a time, times and half a time, out of the serpent's reach.
> Then from his mouth the serpent spewed water like a river, to overtake the woman and sweep her away with the torrent. But the earth helped the woman by opening its mouth and

swallowing the river that the dragon had spewed out of its mouth.

Then the dragon was enraged at the woman and went off to wage war against the rest of her offspring—those who keep God's command and hold fast their testimony about Jesus (Rev.12:13-17)

Before we analyze some of the lines in the preceding quote, note that I did not quote the verses 7-12 which deal with Satan being cast out of heaven to the earth. Why? these verses are reflective not of a future casting down of Satan but the original expulsion from heaven as depicted some OT passages (e.g., Isaiah 14:12-15; Ezek.28 14-17). Satan deceived our ancestral parents in the garden of Eden, that also put his casting out of heaven in the distant past.

The preceding quote (Rev.12:12-17) is a description of Satan's persecution of Israel and by extension the Church. The terminal part of this persecution will be the last three and a half years of the *Great Tribulation* (referred to as time, times, and half a time). Satan's one-world government, a coalition of Gentile nations under the Antichrist will seek to annihilate Israel during the Great Tribulation, but God will not only preserve a remnant from being destroyed, He will rescue Israel.

Israel's Time of Testing

The Testing. *The Great Tribulation* will be a time of testing and preparation of Israel to receive the Messiah, Jesus Christ. As stated earlier, blindness happen in part to the Jews until the fullness of the Gentiles are brought into the kingdom

(Rom.11:25). It is spiritual blindness that has prevented Israel from seeing Jesus as the true Messiah. In His earthly ministry, Jesus charged them with blindness, willful blindness; they did not want to see (John 9:39-41; Matt.23 16-17, 26).

To this day that blindness is in place. There are individual Jews here and there that have embraced Jesus as their true Messiah; they are called, Messianic Jews. But Israel as a nation is still in unbelief and spiritual blindness. They have rejected the Messiah and continue in that state of rejection, blindness, and will remain in that state of unbelief until Jesus comes back.

Jesus said to them, "I have come in my Father's name, and you do not accept me; but if someone else comes in his own name, you will accept him" (John 5:43). Some Jews hate Yeshua so strongly that they will not call His name and will spit on you should you come to them with that name. They do not see their Messiah as human and divine in one person, despite what their scripture says (Isa.7:13-16; 9:6-7).

To them Messiah is a powerful human leader like King David who will restore Israel's pride and honor. The Bible goes on to say, "And for this reason God will send them strong delusion, that they will believe a lie, that they all may be condemned who did not believe the truth but have pleasure in unrighteousness" (2 Thess.2: 11-12). Despite a strong evangelical witness around them, Israel will continue in their state of unbelief or spiritual blindness until Christ's *Second Advent.*

At the beginning of the Great Tribulation, Israel will accept the Satanic imposter, commonly known as the Antichrist, as their long looked for Messiah. To secure Israel's cooperation and confidence, this deceiver will give Israel most favored nation status; that means, Israel is guaranteed economic and military security under a signed treaty or covenant (Dan.9:27).

But three and a half years later, when the Antichrist has consolidated his power and become strong, he will break the treaty with Israel and turn against them. Israel will be forced to worship the beast and receive his number which no sincere Torah believing Jew will do (Rev.13:15-18). This means death!

Gentile nations under the Antichrist will besiege Israel and Jerusalem to annihilate its people. Satan wanted to do this all along, but he could not because the Church was still here, and God would not allow it. But now the Church is gone, removed from the earth to a safe place, spiritual darkness desecends.

So, with the salt and light gone, the restraint on Satan is removed. Satan now thinks he can do as he pleases. Israel appears to be the only nation refusing to submit to the Antichrist's authority based on Torah moral and spiritual values.

Satan's secret agenda all along is to prevent Jesus Christ from fulfilling the covenant with Israel. To fulfill that covenant, Jesus must return to sit on the throne of David and rule over the earth in righteousness and justice from Jerusalem (Isa.9: 6-7). To prevent this from happening, Satan must destroy Jerusalem and the Jewish people. Or at least, pre-emptively occupy Jerusalem through one of his human proxies. But that plan will fail!

Satan's next option is to defeat the Christ in open warfare and prove God a liar (Rev.19:11-16,19-20). Despite his imminent defeat, the Antichrist will slaughter many but will not be able to annihilate Israel. Until the kingdom is restored to Israel, she will go through a time of testing and preparation.

Israelites Time of Preparation

Israel's time of testing is also part of her time of preparation. From human's perspectives, the *Great Tribulation* is a specific time of testing for Israel, but from God's perspective it will be a time of specific spiritual preparation of Israel to receive their Messiah at His second coming. The 144,000 Israelites being sealed is one example of that preparation (Rev.7, 14:1-7).

We do not have to guess who the group of a 144,00 is, because the Bible clearly states that they are Israelites, 12,000 from each of the twelve tribes of Israel. In as much as Bible scholars often speak of the "ten lost tribes of Israel," they are not lost to God, in terms of their geographical whereabouts. God knows exactly where every individual is located. It is foolish, therefore, for anyone to contend that they are loss to history and cannot be regathered for that reason. It is God who is assembling this diversified, multi-ethnic, multi-national group of Israelites from all over the world, not man.

We are often tempted to think that all of Israel are Jews, but they are not. Abraham had several children, and they are not all part of the covenant. The covenant is through Isaac and Jacob (Rom.9: 6-13). There are people that God will identify in this 144,000 that human eyes will never be able identify as Jews. The Bible speaks of "synagogues of Satan" and those "who say they are Jews and are not" (Rev.2:9).

Jehovah's Witnesses falsely teach that the 144,000 is the total number of people redeemed from the earth for heaven and anointed to rule over the new earth.[12] But there are many reasons why that could not be so. I will cite two here as follows.

First, the Bible teaches that all born-again believers are sealed by the blessed Holy Spirit(2 Cor.1: 22; Eph.4: 30). The seal is a sign of ownership, they are God's property, His redeem and children of heaven. For this reason, Satan also have his people sealed with what is called the mark of the beast; it is a mark of Satan's ownership.

Second, the same Revelation 7 (vv.9-17) shows us a multitude separate from the 144,00 that no one could number of all nations, tribes, peoples, and tongues standing before the throne and before the Lamb, clothed with white robes, with palm branches in their hands... They are in heaven, and they came from earth, they are an inclusive group and part of the Church, if not the whole Church. But they are distinct from the 144,000. So that Jehovah's Witness' false teaching dies under its own weight. The 144,000 already embraced Jesus as their Savior, Lord, and Messiah. They are akin to those we refer to as Messianic Jews today.

Some will ask, what is the function of this group, what is their assignment? Most Bible scholars agree that the 144,000 are Israelites, sealed by God from all twelve tribes of Israel as the text of Scripture says. Their assignment is to preach the gospel of salvation to Israel during the *Great Tribulation* period. This is to prepare Israel for their acceptance or rejection of the Messiah when he comes in glory at the near end of the tribulation.

These Jewish evangelists will help strengthen Jewish faith not to accept the false messiah or worship his image or take his mark, but to persevere for deliverance is at hand. The leaders Israel had already accepted the Antichrist at the beginning of the *Great Tribulation* as the likely messiah when they signed the deceptive treaty. That treaty stops short of requiring Israel to take the mark of the beast or worship his image at the time.

But three and a half years later, the treaty is broken, and the mark of the beast, and the worship of the beast are mandatory, and brutally enforced (Rev.13:11-18). Israel knows for sure now that this beast is not the true messiah but Satan in disguise.

The 144,000 Jewish evangelists are preachers to help them keep faith. This 144,000 remnant Jews are protected by God, so the Antichrist cannot hurt them. Israel is given their final chance to come to Yeshua for salvation. The Jesus that their ancestors crucified, and they consistently rejected over two millennia is the true Messiah of Israel. He is underway to sit on the throne of David and reign over the earth form Jerusalem. You must come to faith now; He offers salvation, forgiveness of sin, and eternal life. Most if not all Israel will accept this final offer.

When Jesus returns, and their eye behold Him in glory, the blindness will be fully lifted, and all Israel will be saved because they will clearly see and accept Jesus their true Messiah. But make no mistake, Jews or Gentiles that refused Christ and accepted the mark of the beast or worship his image are lost. There is no salvation apart from a relationship with Jesus Christ. This point is further developed in chapter 7.

The path from unbelief to acceptance will be painful, but not without purpose; it prepares the nation to stand firm under trial to receive the true Messiah. Like the three Hebrew boys in Babylon, they will be rescued from the burning fiery furnace after having gone through it. The next chapter shows how Israel is rescued from annihilation by the Messiah.

CHAPTER 3

THE RESCUE OF ISRAEL

Israel will be rescued from annihilation. The Antichrist's forces, a coalition of nations, will besiege Israel; its military mission is to annihilate Israel. The reason for this annihilation has been stated several times already; it is to destroy the Jewish State and prevent the return of the Jewish Messiah, Jesus Christ.

Israel has been in Satan's crosshairs through all of history, and many nations have tried to exterminate the Jews before, but they are a resilient people and refused to go away.

They are God's covenant people and God must fulfill His covenant with them, despite their unfaithfulness. Satan wants to destroy Israel to prevent their Messiah, Jesus Christ, the Son of Man, the Son of God from returning to sit on the throne of David and rule over the earth in righteousness and justice from Jerusalem (Isa.9:6-7).

Armageddon is Satan's best chance to achieve that object. The Church has left earth to heaven, so Satan's restraint is lifted, and the economic resources of all nations with their collective nuclear arsenal are under Satan's control. Satan's human faces are the Antichrist and the False prophet, the twin beasts of Revelation 13. Satan has never been so well positioned to get what he wants since he was expelled from heaven.

But he has one more river to cross, and that is to prevent Jesus from returning to reign. That is heavy lifting for Satan because he is not omnipotent; his effort is raw arrogance and defiance. He reasoned that if Israel is destroyed, then there is no reason for Jesus to come back, for there is no covenant promise to hold true to—if there is no land, there is no kingdom to rule over. Jesus can setup shop somewhere else; there is a big universe out there, after all. That's Satan's flawed reasoning.

Satan tricked Adam and Eve out of their rightful governance of the earth and setup himself as god of this world. But Adam and Eve were tenants and caretakers of the earth, not its owner (Gen.1:26-28, 2:15; Ps.8: 3-9). God is the owner and holder of the title deed to the earth (Ps.24:1). Satan will be expelled at the time appointed by God; Israel is part of that expulsion plan, and Satan knows it, and seeks to put out her light.

But Israel is a burning flame, not very easy to extinguish! Egypt tried, Assyria tried, Babylon tried, Persia tried, Rome tried, Nazi Germany tried, and in the face of all that, Israel returns as a nation State in 1948. She is a thriving State, but is still hated by several nations, including her neighbors.

Satan is now going to do what other devils could not do, try to annihilate Israel by all necessary means. It is for this reason the great Gentiles powers are now united to do. They have all the available resources of the earth under their command, everything to achieve their military objectives. The operation is called, Armageddon. The Psalmist speaks prophetically, "The kings of the earth rise up and the rulers band together against the Lord and against his anointed...but the One enthroned in heavens laughs; the Lord scoffs at them"(Psalm 2:1-4).

The Moved to Annihilate Israel

While the Gentile powers of earth under the leadership and influence of the Antichrist and Satan convene nations for war to annihilate Israel, God is at work behind the scenes as this drama unfolds. The apostle John in Revelation (16:12-16) gives us the following intelligence report:

> The sixth angel poured out his bowl [of wrath] on the great river Euphrates, and the water was dried up to prepare the way for the kings from the East. Then I saw three unclean spirits that looked like frogs; they came out of the mouth of the dragon, out of the mouth of the beast and out of the mouth of the false prophet. They are demon spirits that perform signs, and they go out to the kings of the whole world, to gather them for battle on the great day of God Almighty…. Then they gathered the kings together to the place that in Hebrew is called Armageddon. (Rev.16:12-14, 16).

The preceding quote brings us to a point in the second half of the seven-years of *Great Tribulation*. Note that it is the unholy trinity: Satan (the dragon), the beast (the Antichrist), and the False prophet with their cohorts of demons that are calling world leaders and their armies from the East to march across the Euphrates to join other armies to besiege Israel in that which is known as the *Armageddon war campaign*.

Again, note the three froglike demon spirits coming from the mouths of Satan, the Antichrist, and the false prophet. Demons do influence leaders of nations to do Satan's bidding. That is one reason believers are commanded to pray for the leaders of the secular State (1Tim.2:1-4). Many leaders are under the influence of territorial angels, demons assigned by Satan.

Remember, at the time of this military march to annihilate Israel, the true Church of believers has already gone from the earth. The salt and light Church is gone; Satan and his human proxies are in charge of world government, the economy, the militaries, and everything else. But just as other attempts to destroy Israel failed, so will this one. But even though it is destined to fail, thousands of Jews will suffer loss of life but not necessarily the loss of eternal life.

Satan and his human proxies, the Antichrist and the false prophet are clearly at work in this wicked scheme; they are bringing their total military assets and forces in one place, to besiege Israel and Jerusalem, then annihilate its people. This is perhaps, Satan's second colossal mistake since his expulsion from heaven. Armageddon is a divine setup to permanently destroy Satan's operation. God in His Sovereignty is at work to bring the arm forces of the Antichrist to ruin.

The Great Battle of God Almighty

The Armageddon War campaign is spoken of innumerous scripture passages; we can only name a few here. The apostle John calls this Armageddon gathering, "the battle of the great day of God Almighty" (Rev.16:14). It is God who summons Satan, the Antichrist, the false prophet, and Gentile nations with their arm forces and leaders to deal with them at this location concerning His people, Israel. But Satan and his human proxies think it is their own doing.

The battles of the Armageddon campaign will be fought, perhaps in several locations, but over the same issue from God's perspective, "my people Israel." The prophet Joel describes for us God's intensions as follows:

> In those days and at that time, when I restore the fortunes of Judah and Jerusalem, I will gather all nations and bring them down to the Valley of Jehoshaphat. There I will put them on trial for what they did to my inheritance, my people Israel, because they scattered my people among the nations and divided up my land. They cast lots for my people and traded boys for prostitutes; they sold girls for wine to drink. (Joel 3:1-3)

The preceding quote from Joel chapter 3 tells us God is the one gathering the nations to that location and why. They are marching there to carry out the hate in their own hearts toward Israel but at the same time, they are fulfilling prophecy. And God is going to use the occasion to judge the nations and bring them to utter ruin. The Valley of Jehoshaphat is said to be "an extended area east of Jerusalem."[1]

The prophet Ezekiel (chapters 37-39) also speaks of the regathering of the people of Israel and the gathering of the Gentile nations to this region where God will deal with them in judgment. The leader Gog and the nation Magog of Revelation (20:7) refers to the Antichrist with his allied nations coming against Israel. God will destroy them (Ezek.38-39).

Jerusalem will be the chief center of conflict; it is the prize that Satan wants above all else, because it is the City of God, the place where the Messiah will rule from upon His return. Satan and his proxy, the Antichrist, are making a preemptive strike on Jerusalem to make it Satan's city and the place of his throne. That's what the Gentiles powers are doing in Satan's name. But this is what God says about Jerusalem in Zechariah 12:

> I am going to make Jerusalem a cup that sends all the surrounding people reeling. Judah will be besieged as well as Jerusalem. On that day, when all nations of the earth are gathered against her, I will make Jerusalem an immovable rock for all nations. All who try to move it will injure themselves. On that day I will strike every horse with panic and its rider with madness.... I will keep a watchful eye over Judah, but I will blind all the horses of the nations. 'Then the clans of Judah will say in their hearts, The people of Jerusalem are strong, because the LORD Almighty is their God.' (Zech.12: 2-5)

In the preceding quote, note the difficulty Jerusalem will cause for nations who seek to tamper with her—she sends them "reeling." Like an immobile stone hurt those trying to move it, so will Jerusalem hurt those nations that seek to move her. It is a warning from God to leave Jerusalem alone; it is the City of God. Over the years, the United States and the United Kingdom Have been the primary supporters of Israel, defending her right to exist as a State in peace and security. That does not mean that all US administrations and Prime Ministers of Great Britain have seen eye to eye with the leaders of Israel, not at all. There have been times when promises made were not kept; some refer to such reversals as "betrayal" of Israel.[2]

For example, Great Britain under the Balfour Declaration of 1917 agreed to the full support of the Jewish State in Palestine. The Declaration partly reads, "His Majesty's Government views with favor the establishment in Palestine of a national home for the Jewish people and will use their best endeavors to facilitate the achievement of this object..."[3] But when the time came to enforce the Declaration, Britain cave-in to political pressure.

Some have argued that the Balfour Declaration was made upon understanding agreed to in the Versailles Conference, which states the Jewish people's historic right to the land and to the extent of it, which would include, Trans-Jordan. But Britain later reneged on their promise, cutting off a large swath of the land in 1922 which was Israel's, to form the nation that is now, Jordan.[4]

This partial reversal of the Balfour Declaration is seen as a betrayal of Israel. Notwithstanding, Great Britain and the United are, at least, two nations that do not deny Israel's right to exist and will defend her militarily if necessary.

The major powers have pressured Israel to surrender land for peace. This is hard for Israel to do because God Himself gave the land to Israel and defined its borders (Joshua 1:1-6). At times, pressure and negotiation brought Israel close to agreeing to a Palestinian State, then the whole thing falls apart. At the publishing of this book, there was little or no talk of a two-state solution in the public media. Several leaders that championed this cause have died and the problem remains. Everybody wants to lay claim to Jerusalem, but God says, it is mine! Jerusalem remains the immovable stone.

Look again at the preceding quote from Zachariah 12 and note the words, "I will strike every horse with panic and its rider with madness." What does this mean? The time the prophecy was written, the horse was the mode of transportation to war and war was fought on land. This means, God will cause problems with all mechanized war transportation that come against Israel: land vehicles, mobilized racket launchers, tanks, and the like. Their drivers will lose their minds and go mad.

The prophecy also says, "I will blind the horses." Here again the horse is used for transportation, but in our time, air transportation. All engines, even fighter jets, including drones are made up of horsepower, but a pilot sees by using navigation instruments, including radars. If these instruments are not working, we say the pilot is flying blind, that spells disaster for the pilot and his machine. That is what is meant by, "I will blind the horses."

Satan and his Gentile proxy nations that will besiege Israel, killing its people, and putting the strangle hold on Jerusalem, will be fighting against God Himself. The Antichrist's military mission is the utter annihilation of Israel, but God will not allow them to achieve their military purpose for Satan. Why not?

Satan is mighty, but God is Almighty and intends to destroy their military machine and bring them to judgment. Israel will play its final card; they will cry out to God for help!

The Fight and Rescue

The cry comes up to heaven just about the time the Church is finishing the *Marriage Supper* celebration banquet (Rev.19:6-9).

Remember, the invasion of Israel takes place in the intensity of the last half of *Great Tribulation*, as it is counting down to its end. Jesus is already scheduled to return to earth with His Church at the near end of the seven years of *Great Tribulation* (Matt.24:29-31; Jude 14). This return to earth is the *Second Coming of the Christ*. The apostle John gives us a picturesque description of this event happening in real time:

> I saw heaven standing open and there before me was a white horse, whose rider is called Faithful and True. With justice he judges and wages war.
>
> His eyes are like blazing fire, and on his head are many crowns. He has a name written on him that no one knows but he himself. He is dressed in a rob dipped in blood, and his name the Word of God. The armies of heaven were following him,

riding on white horses and dressed in fine linen, white and clean.

Coming from his mouth is a sharp sword with which to strike down the nations. He will rule them with an iron scepter. He treads the winepress of the fury of the wrath of God Almighty. On his robe and on his thigh he has this name written: KING of Kings AND LORD OF LORDS. (Rev.19:11-16)

The preceding quote speaks for itself. It depicts Jesus Christ returning on a milk white war horse; he is in fury, burning with holy rage to execute justice and judgment. Only Israel is happy to see Him for He comes to rescue them. But the nations' war machines are in place, prepared to cut Him down in their fury with their advance weapons as soon as He is in sight. But that is easier said than done; the Bible teach that "many are the plans in man's heart, but it is the purpose of God that prevails."

The eastern sky will split asunder and in blazing, blinding, dazzling glory, brighter than the midday sun Jesus will descend to earth with an army of saints and angels. The prophet Zechariah picks up His landing, "On that day his feet will stand on the Mount of Olives, east of Jerusalem, and the Mount of Olives will be split in two from east to west, forming a great valley, with half of the mountain moving north and half moving south" (Zech.14: 3-4). And "the battle of [the] great day of God Almighty" has begun (Rev.16:14). Satan and his human proxies, the Antichrist and the false prophet think it's their doing, it's their war to accomplish their wicked purpose. But it is God who summons the kings of the earth to war to destroy them.

The Outcome of the War

The armies of the earth proved to be no match for Jesus Christ who sits on the white horse. With the sharp sword of His mouth (His Word) He cuts down millions of the enemy's forces and destroys their war machines. He captures their leaders, the Antichrist, and the false prophet, and throws them alive into the lake of burning sulfur which is hell (Rev.19:19-21).

Satan, the spiritual commander behind this war operation is later taken into custody (Rev.20:1-3). And Israel is rescued from utter annihilation, and Jesus returns from the war victorious, not losing as much as one person. The prophet Isaiah gives us a prophetic description of this victory. He writes:

> Who is this coming from Edom, from Bozrah, with his garments stained crimson? Who is this, robed in splendor, striding forward in the greatness of his strength?
>
> It is I, proclaiming victory, mighty to save. Why is your garments red, like those of one treading the winepress? I have trodden the winepress alone: from the nations no one was with me.
>
> I trampled them in my anger, and I trod them down in my wrath; their blood spattered my garments, and I stained all my clothing. It was for

me the day of vengeance; the year for me to redeem had come.

I looked, but there was no one to help, I was appalled that no one gave me support; so my own arm wrath achieved salvation for me; and my own wrath sustained me. I trampled the nations in my anger in my wrath I made them drunk and poured their blood on the ground. (Isaiah 63:1-6)

The implication of the preceding passage is that the fighting was singularly done by the rider on the white horse which is Jesus Christ. Even though He returns to earth with an army of saints and angels, it appears as if He did not require them to fight. He did not have to fight with human weapons. His word is His weapon of war. "The word of God is alive and active. Sharper than any double-edged sword, it penetrates even to dividing of soul and spirit, joints and marrow..." (Heb.12:4).

Jesus is the Logos, the Word that brings things int existence and give them life (John 1:1-1-4, 14). By extension, He can speak things, all life, out of existence. It appears that is what takes place in this Armageddon war.

If the saints and angels that accompany Jesus from heaven are required to fight, you can understand why they would not sustain any casualties—neither Jesus nor those with can die. Jesus already conquered death in His first advent and dies no more (1 Cor.15:20; Rom.6:9; Heb.7:24). Secondly, the saints with him are in their glorified state, and like Him cannot die again (Rom.8:29-30; 1Cor.15:51-57). In the third place, angels are spirit beings; humans cannot kill them, they are not mortals.

Look again at preceding Isaiah 63 quote; it has two ironies worth contemplating. First, it is the very opposite of Isaiah 53, which vividly describes our Lord's life and death during His first advent to this earth. He was the suffering servant of God, the substitutionary sacrifice, the Lamb of God whose life was given for our redemption. He was beaten, crucified; His blood ran lazily down the parched earth of Golgotha at high noon on that first Good Friday. He was dying not for Himself, but for the redemption of humankind (John3:16).

Those who crucified Him knew He was innocent, that includes Caiaphas, and Pilate, the Roman governor (John 18:29-40, 19:1-16). Nonetheless, Jesus prayed for their forgiveness then, but they still rejected Him. After two thousand years, Jews continue their rejection of Jesus, the Christ.

The second irony, when He returns to earth, after so long a time, the nations of the earth will be ready to fight Him, not one will come to His defense, according to the prophetic forecast. Note the words, "I looked, but there was no one to help, I was appalled that no one gave me support…" (Isa.63:5).

The man who gave His life for all humankind is not welcome to the earth He created; the tenants are ready to kill Him. Perhaps, you can now see why He is so furious in Isaiah 63; He tramples upon His enemies as one stamping upon grapes in a winepress, thus His garment is stained red, not with grapes but with blood. Armageddon is His "day of vengeance" (v.4).

Armageddon's Aftermath

War is a messy business; cleanup is necessary after each one. The Armageddon war will result in millions of dead bodies all over the place. A massive cleaning up by burying, burning, and other methods will be deployed to prevent disease.

The apostle John records one of the cleanup methods arranged by the Lord Jesus before the war. John writes, "And I saw an angel standing in the sun, who cried in a loud voice to all the birds flying in midair, 'Come gather together for the great supper of God, so that you may eat the flesh of kings, generals, and of mighty men, of horses, and their riders, and the flesh of all people, free and slave, great and small'" (Rev.19:17-18).

Some of the nations that come against Israel that will be destroyed are Magog and allies (Ezek.38-39). Scholars have identified Magog as Russia which is a strong possibility. But the Magog of Revelation is not necessarily the Magog of Ezekiel.

Whether they are the same is not our concern here. The fact is—the nations will be allied with the Antichrist and will come against Israel and will be destroyed. The death told will be in the millions and will take months to cleanup.

These armies will be buried in Israel, and many will be burnt to prevent disease. Ezekiel writes, "It will come to pass in that day that I will give Gog a burial place there in Israel, the Valley of those who pass by east of the sea; and it will obstruct travelers, because there they will bury Gog and his multitudes.... For seven months the house of Israel will be burying them, in order to clean up the land" (Ezek.39:11-12).

Perhaps not in this order, but Israel is rescued, the land is cleaned up, Israel is judge and restored (Ezek.39:21-29). The time of the Gentiles has permanently come to its end with Christ's Armageddon victory. From here onward, the form of government on earth will be theocracy. It is the complete fulfillment of Isaiah's prophecy:

> For to us a child is born, to us a son is given, and the government will be on his shoulders. And he will be called Wonderful Counselor, Mighty God, Everlasting Father, Prince of Peace. Of the greatness of his government and peace there will be no end. He will reign on David's throne and over his kingdom, establishing and upholding it with justice and righteousness from that time and forever. The zeal of the LORD Almighty will accomplish this. (Isa.9:6-7)

Summary

The average Christian today knows very little of Israel's history beyond what they learned in Sunday School. They do not know of the political struggles the Jewish people have gone through to bring about the rebirth of the modern Jewish state of Israel or the biblical and prophetic connections between a functional Jewish State and the Second Coming of the Christ.

It should be strongly emphasized, therefore, that for the preceding Scripture (Isa.9:6-7) to be fulfilled—first, there must be a functional Jewish State in place for the Messiah to rule over; that functional State already in place. This signals that the rapture of the Church is nearer than most Christians realize, therefore, readiness for that event cannot be over emphasized.

Second, the regathering of the Jewish people from among the nations and the move to restore the Jews to their historic homeland have been going on from the late 19th century and became more prominent under the name, Zionism.

Third, in as much as there is a functional Jewish State since 1948, the regathering of the Jews is not complete, and will not be completed until Messiah is revealed from heaven in His second advent and rescue Israel from annihilation. At that time the 10 loss tribes of Israel will be more accurately identified, and those who falsely claim to be Jews exposed.

Israel will be indicted and judged. In fact, Israel has been under indictment throughout her rebellious history. Chapter 4 partly looks at that indictment from Scripture. Israel will then be judged. Just as Christians has a believers' judgment that they must stand before the judgment seat of Christ, so Jews rescued at the time of Christ Second Advent from the Antichrist will face judgment before they enter the Millennium.

All Jews that embrace Yeshua as their Messiah will be saved, perhaps the entire nation or what's left of it, the remnant. They will witness the Davidic Kingdom restored with the Messiah sitting on David's throne (Isa.9:6-7). The Gentiles nations will also face judgment to determine which nations enters the millennial kingdom of the Christ (Matt.25:31-56).

CHAPTER 4
ISRAEL'S INDICTMENT

The chapter after this one deals with God's judgment or trial of Israel as in a court of law. The natural thing to ask is, what is the indictment or charged against Israel? Israel is guilty of breach of covenant. In the modern world we are more familiar with breach of contract; it is the closest relational agreement to a covenant. A marriage agreement is the closest contract in our time to a biblical covenant; it is a legal transaction, and when it is breached it becomes a matter for the courts.

In fact, churches solemnizing matrimony recognize it as a covenant before God, in which He bears witness. That is one reason it is preposterous and even blasphemous to ask God to bless a matrimonial covenant relationship that is not after the divine order instituted in Genesis (1:27-28, 2:21-25).

The word covenant comes from the Hebrew word, *b^{e}rit*, which means, "to cut," and it denotes various transactions done in the ancient world between God and humans, as well as between fellow humans (e.g., tribes, nations, individuals) in which each party bound himself to fulfill certain obligations and received the advantages promised (1Sam.11:1, Jos.9:6, 15; Gen.21:27).[1] "In the making of a covenant, God was solemnly invoked as a witness," and "an oath was sworn" (Gen.31:53, 21:31). This resulted in the expression, "a covenant of the Lord" (1 Sam.20:8; Jer.34:18-19; Ezek.17:19).[2]

So, in Bible times, when two parties formed a binding agreement, they were cutting an agreement, thus it was called, a covenant. The ceremony would involve the sacrificing of an animal, in the case of a blood covenant (Gen.15: 9-21).

In the preceding Scripture reference (Gen.15), note how Abraham was commanded by God to cut the sacrifice in pieces, lay them before the Lord, and walk between the pieces. The significance here is—if the covenant is breached, may the guilty party be cut in pieces in like manner. The breach of covenant was considered a very serious sin (Ezek.17:12-20).

Furthermore, for Abraham and his descendants, the cutting was made on the foreskin of the reproductive organ of the male and referred to as "circumcision." So, the sign of the covenant was carried in the body of each male Israelite under this binding obligation or covenant (Gen.17:1-27).

Marriage agreement in Bible times was a covenant before God (Prov.2:17). As such, it has not changed; it is still a covenant today. Jesus affirms its sanctity and permanence in the Sermon on the Mount (Matt.5: 31-32). A good marriage is the most joyful and intimate relationship on earth. In the Old Testament (OT), God used marriage to illustrate His covenant relationship with His people, Israel (Isa.54:5, 63: 4-5; Jer.3:1; Hos.2:16-20). Like Israel, in the New Testament (NT), the relationship between Christ and His Church is also illustrated with the covenant of marriage (Eph.5: 21-33).

In the Old Testament, God's covenant relationship with Israel started with Abraham but was formally entered into under Moses at Saini with the whole nation (Exod.19: 3-8; 34: 10-28). Israel said, yes to the terms of the covenant, and once you say yes to God, that becomes a binding oath or vow.

Just like a marriage, God's covenant relationship requires faith and fidelity. In a marriage, one party normally takes the name of the other. In like manner, God refers to Himself as the God of Abraham, Isaac, and Jacob. Israel's unfaithfulness to God is referred to as adultery or prostitution or harlotry (Isa.1:21; Jer.2:20; Hos.1-3). God's constant problem with Israel was idolatry, spiritual prostitution, a sin, and a "political crime" (Deut.17:2-5).[3]

Covenant Renewed

The covenant at Sinai with Israel under Moses is, on the one hand, a renewal of the Abrahamic covenant, while on the other hand new and more extensive. Perhaps, better stated, it is the continued fulfillment of the covenant made with Abraham.

Since, the generation that said, yes to God at Sinai failed to enter the land because of idolatry, disobedience, and unbelief,

Moses had to renew the covenant with the new generation in Deuteronomy. "Deuteronomy" means, second law because the Law was given a second time to the younger generation. This generation inherited the land under Joshua (Jos.1:1-8).

Because Israel was so unfaithful living up to the terms of the covenant, God promised to raise up a prophet like Moses from among the people, and to enact a new covenant (Jer.31:31-36). A main feature of the new covenant is that law of God would be written inwardly on the hearts of His people, instead of externally on tables of stone. And the Spirit of God would indwell the people of God, giving them the capability to keep God's law. The old law was more of a signpost; it pointed Israel to their destination, but it could not take them there.

The prophet like Moses God would raise up from among the people would be the Messiah who would come through the royal line of King David. God promised David that someone, a Son from his linage would sit on his throne. That person would be the Messiah, Jesus Christ (Isa.9: 6-7). The Messiah came but Israel rejected Him, but the Gentiles received Him (John 1:12).

The Gentiles were brought under the blessings of the New Covenant because they believed God. The New Covenant gives more than a piece of land flowing with milk and honey; it gives eternal life. But that eternal life is resident in the Son of God, Jesus Christ (John 3:14-16). To reject Him is to reject life, eternal life (vv.18-21). When Messiah comes again, He will judge Israel for their unbelief just as gentiles that reject Him will be judged. And at that time, the Messiah will fulfill the covenant to Israel made to David.

Israel's Breach of Covenant

The first sweeping charge against Israel is breach of covenant; the legal agreement between them and Jehovah was violated. They accepted Jehovah as the one true God and pledged themselves faithfully in service to Him but breach that trust (Exod.19:3-8;20:2-5). They did not keep faith; Israel's idolatry from Judges to Malachi is stunning.

They have offended God, sinned against Him, violated divine law, and a just and holy God must hold them accountable to the terms of the covenant (Deut.28). Their idolatry is documented throughout the Old Testament, which can serve as a legal brief against them in judgment. The first and second commandments are specifically against idolatry (Exod.20: 1-4).

The second sweeping charge against Israel is their willful rejection of the Son of God, their Messiah (John 1:12). They set aside the written revelation of God and substituted their own man-made tradition for the Word of God. Blinded by their own sins, they were unable to recognize the Son of Man among them. Their leaders had Him executed on a Roman cross and covered up the truth of His resurrection.

Israel Is Under Indictment

Israel is under divine indictment on the two broad counts of breach of covenant stated in the previous section: 1) their constant idolatry, and 2) their continued rejection of Jesus Christ, the Messiah. Just as all believers and unbeliever must face judgment, Israel is accountable to God, and must face judgment before they enter their inheritance.

Israel's indictment is seen through the Scriptures, Old and New Testament. The OT sums it up in one word, idolatry or unfaithfulness or disobedience. In the NT it is rejection of the Messiah, sometimes called blindness, the establishment of their own truth or righteousness (Rom.2-3). In this section, we will just refer to a few passages where this indictment can be seen.

The foundational text in the Toral that lays down the penalty for adultery or unfaithful or disobedience toward God and the covenant is Deuteronomy 28:15-68; the first part of the chapter (vv.1-14) states the blessings or benefits for abiding by the terms of the covenant. The blessings are comprehensive, far-reaching, and exceedingly generous. The curses are the very opposite.

The book of Isaiah is replete with God's indictment of Israel. Here God sits as judge against the nation, and calls heaven and earth to bear witness:

> Hear me, you heavens! Listen, earth! For the LORD has spoken: I reared children and brought them up. The ox knows its master, the donkey its owner's manger, but Israel does not know, my people do not understand.
> Woe to the sinful nation, a people whose guilt is great, a brood of evildoers, children given to corruption! They have forsaken the LORD; they have spurned the Holy One of Israel and turn their backs on him…. (Isaiah 1:2-4).

The entire chapter one of Isaiah's prophecy is a litany of charges; it describes the spiritually sick condition of the nation. "From the sole of your foot to the top of your head there is no soundness—

only wounds and welts and open sores, not cleaned or bandaged or soothed with olive oil" (v.6).

The book of Hosea is an illustration of God's covenant relationship with His people Israel; His love is steadfast despite Israel's unfaithfulness. The prophet's marriage depicts in vivid terms God love, Israel infidelity or idolatry, God's indictment of their idolatry, His forgiveness and restoration of the nation to Himself. The indictment and judgment come in Hosea chapter 4, and restoration in chapter 11.

The prophet Malachi records this indictment as well, and this is very significant because he is the last of the old order. John the Baptist is a transitional figure who introduces the new order of things. There are 400 years between these two prophets: Malachi and John the Baptist

Malachi prophesied during a time of Israel's backsliding; the nation was in a breach of covenant, and blaming their troubles on God, that He abandoned them because He did not love them. Like other prophets, Malachi addressed matters relevant to the spiritual condition of his time. But his prophecy also has relevance for the future of Israel, and implications for the larger covenant community, because it reveals the nature of God's character and how He works, His expectation and the like.

The prophet uses a rhetorical, question and answer style. God declares His covenant love for Israel, and Israel questions that love. "I have loved you," says the Lord. "But you ask, 'How have you loved us?' (Mal.1:2). He goes on to lay out God's indictment to the nation, using their own words back to them, mirroring back their thoughts and attitudes (2:14,17, 3:7-8,13-

15). He indicted the priesthood, showing if they refuse to repent God would curse them and remove them from service.

Malachi also announces a future day of judgment and justice; God will come to judge as a refiner's fire (2:17, 4:1-5). John the Baptist picks up on this theme of judgment, justice, and cleansing in his preaching (Matt.3:10-13).

Israel is under indictment and judgment for a long time. It started in the Old Testament and should have ended with the first coming of the Messiah, but Israel rejected the Messiah, thus postponed and prolonging the time of their redemption, and lengthens their indictment and judgment. At the second advent they will be judge face to face and the nation will be restored.

Has Israel Been Cast Away?

Despite their breach of covenant, indictment, and judgment long before the Church age and during the Church age, God has not cast away or abandoned or replace His covenant people. They have been temporary set aside while in their state of blindness, disobedience, and unbelief (Rom. 9-11).

Israel is still being blessed materially under the old covenant, but that blessing eclipse what Israel would have been had they not rejected the Messiah. They would have been the number one nation on earth, the go to power for all nations, the head and not the tail.

At the second advent of the Christ, Yeshua will rescue them from their enemies, remove their blindness, and they will embrace him as their Messiah. He will judge them face to face, and the kingdom will be restored to Israel; that is time, God has set by His own authority (Acts 1:6-7).

CHAPTER 5

THE JUDGMENT OF ISRAEL

In Volume 2 of this series, it is stated that at a minimum, Jesus Christ operates in four offices: Prophet, Priest, King, and Judge. But we tend to push His office of Judge to the time of His Second Advent, hence, we often speak of Him coming to judge the "quick and the dead" as stated in some of the oldest creeds of the Church, such as the apostles' creed.[1]

But the fact is, our Lord Jesus Christ is very much active as judge now in the Church age as depicted in Paul's exhortation to the Corinthians on the abuse of the Lord's Supper and John's letter to the seven churches (1 Cor.11:29-32; Rev.2-3). But note that His judgments now are more corrective, than punitive. The judgment to come is punitive.[2]

There are many judgments in the Bible that our Lord is the sitting Judge: the Believers' Judgment, the judgment of Israel, the judgment of nations, and the final judgment, to name a few. We call them judgments but in fact they are judgment sessions. Judgment sessions are functions of the Supreme Court of God's Kingdom; sessions are convened at different time and place.

The focus of this chapter is the judgment of Israel. But again, I want to paint in broad strokes, that means less details. Because of the glut of scriptural material devoted to Israel and her dynamic history, it appears as if Israel is always under judgment, and in fact, she is as the previous chapter indicates. Of course, the previous chapter is more focused on indictment.

The Scriptural Basis

Based on Deuteronomy 28, a strong argument can be made that Israel has reneged on the Mosaic covenant and is under the judgment of God, and the rejection of Jesus Christ, the Messiah, further compounds that judgment.

But this chapter is more focused on the end-time, face to face judgment of Israel with their Messiah Jesus Christ that will take place at His Second Advent.

One question that was always on the minds of Jesus' disciples is the question relating to the time God would restore the Davidic Kingdom to Israel. They asked this question repeatedly but in different ways. The last time the question was asked, appears to be on Ascension Day. Jesus said to them, "It is not for you to know the time or date the Father has set by his own authority" (Acts 1:6-8).

The answer to the question is somewhat vague but very much in keeping with the answer Jesus gave when asked about the date and time of His return (Matt.24:3,36). The answer to both questions is classified. The implication, however, is that they are both eschatological, happening at the end of the age.

It is now clear from scripture that the kingdom that will be restored to Israel is what Bible scholars call, the millennial kingdom (Isa.9:6-7; Rev.20:1-3, 7). That is the time Christ will rule over the earth as KING of Kings and LORD of Lords from Jerusalem. Jerusalem is the city of God.

If that be so, the full regathering of Israel to their covenant land must take place by then. As indicated earlier, that regathering has been underway since the late 19th century, if not earlier. God has been very much at work calling out His people from among the nations and bringing them back to their historic homeland as prophesied long ago.

There are those who postulate that the regathering of Israel will begin after the *Great Tribulation,* after the Armageddon war, but that calculation is at best mistaken. The regathering of Israel began many decades ago, about the late 19th Century.

Significant to the regathering process is the birth of the modern State of Israel in 1948. This regathering will be perfected or brought to its completion at the Second Advent of the Christ, sometime after the Armageddon war.

The instrument to finetune or complete the regathering after the Armageddon rescue is the *Judgment of Israel*. You may ask, why is that so? Four important reasons come to mind:

(1) Israel has been long under indictment for their breach of covenant; now they must face the judge.

(2) The identity of the true Israelite must be sought out. There are people who say they are Jews, and they are not. Jesus refers to them as false Jews or as "synagogues of Satan" (Rev.2:9). The people of the covenant are connected to Abraham through his son Isaac. Abraham had several sons, but they do not come under the covenant (Gen.25:1-6).

(3) *The Ten Lost Tribes of Israel* must be fully identified. They have been scattered amongst the nations; only God knows their identity. It must also be pointed out that there has always been a group of indigenous Jews who never left Palestine.

(4) The Judgment upon Israel will determine who enters the millennial kingdom of the Christ. Furthermore, if anyone bearing the mark of the beast, he or she is a child of Satan and will not be allowed to enter the millennial kingdom.

The Judgment of Israel

Some have suggested the following Scripture passage as referring to the judgment of Israel, but I will show you why it is not so, even though the timing seems prefect.

> I saw thrones on which were seated those who had been given authority to judge. And I saw the souls of those who had been beheaded because of their testimony of about Jesus and because of the word of God. They had not worshiped the beast or its image and had not received its mark on their foreheads or their hands. They came to life and reigned with Christ a thousand years. (Rev.20::4)

The people in the passage are not Old Testament saints, and the passage does not represent the judgment upon Israel. The passage clearly tells who these people are; they were beheaded by the beast (antichrist), because of their testimony of Jesus and the word of God, and because they refused to worship the beast or his image, and they refused to take his mark. The only time the antichrist has the power to do this is during the seven years of Great Tribulation. So, who are they?

They are clearly martyrs of the Great Tribulation; they were killed late in the second half of the tribulation, not in time to join that earlier group that was resurrected to join their fellow saints in heaven for the Marriage of the Lamb and Marriage Supper celebration (Rev.7:9-15). As a group, they are not national Israel, but people who embraced Jesus and were killed. The group could be very much a mixed multitude of Jews and Gentiles that resisted the worship of the beast or taking his ID and were killed.

The Judgment of Israel is face-to face before Jesus; it will not include resurrection of any dead, separate from those spoken of in (Rev.20:4). Old Testament (OT) saints would have been resurrected at the time of the rapture, not at the judgment upon Israel as some scholars would have us believe. Jews and Gentiles who take the mark of the beast or worship his image and are still alive after Armageddon will be judge, and not allowed to enter the millennium to reign with Christ.

Jew that did not accept the mark of the beast or worship his image and embrace Jesus as Savior and Lord will be judged by Christ just as Christian believers were judged in heaven at the Judgment Seat of Christ. Embracing Jesus does not exempt a person from judgment. In the Church age, believers who appear before the judgment seat of Christ will not be judged for their sins but for their works. We cannot say if the judgment of Israel will follow that order; their circumstances are different.

Most of national Israel that Jesus rescue from annihilation, will not have the mark of the beast, not because they suddenly believed in Jesus, but the fact that Israel had a treaty with the Antichrist that exempted them from that requirement. But now the treaty is broken, that exemption no longer applies. Like everybody else, they are forced to worship the beast and take his mark. But Jews steadfastly refused because the Torah forbids the worship of anyone other than Yahweh. It for this reason the Antichrist targeted Israel for annihilation.

Let's take as second go at this. The fact that Israel was granted favored nation status by a signed treaty at the beginning of the *Great Tribulation*, they would not be forced to worship the beast or his image or take his mark until late in the second half of the tribulation when the treaty is broken.

Israel would not have signed a treaty that cause them to throw the Torah and the entire Tanach in the trashcan and worship a man or his image. They would prefer another holocaust to doing such a thing. Example of this stubbornness is the three Hebrew boys in Babylon; they chose the furnace of fire over worshipping the king's image. Yes, a few who don't take their faith seriously will do it, but a whole nation will not do it.

So, most Jews that practice their religion will not take the mark of the beast or worship the Antichrist or his image; that will be a sizable population. That will provoke the Antichrist to be more furious and move to annihilate them on a fast track. But before the Antichrist achieves this goal of annihilation, Jesus will return in the clouds of glory and put an end to the Antichrist's military campaign.

The judgment of Israel will take place sometime after the war of Armageddon, but before they are allowed to enter the millennium. Some scholars think the parable of the ten virgins and the parable of talents refer exclusively to the judgment upon Israel (Matt.25:1-30). In as much as they fall in the context of Jesus' Olivet prophetic teaching on His second coming, I don't see how they could apply exclusively to the judgment of Israel.

The two parables are best viewed and understood as general teaching on the kingdom in relation to the second coming of the Lord. At the time this teaching was given, Jesus knew Israel had fully rejected Him. And now He is instructing the leaders of the Church whose membership would be both Jews and Gentiles. People who unwaveringly believe in dispensationalism, will see the two parables as exclusively Jews because it fits into a theological system they have invented.

Who Are the Judges?

Who will judge Israel? The Chief Judge will be Jesus Christ Himself. He will be assisted by at least the twelve apostles. How do we know that? Jesus asserts that "the Father judges no one, but has entrusted all judgments to the Son, that all may honor the Son as they honor the Father..." (John 5:22-23).

The apostles also speak of Jesus as "the one whom God appointed as judge of the living and the dead" (Acts 10:42). Jesus is referred to as "the righteous judge" who will award crowns of righteousness at His coming (2 Tim.4:8). There are at least two references as to who will assist Jesus in the judging process at His *Second Coming*.

First, His twelve apostles will assist Him. on one occasion Jesus made this statement to the twelve disciples,"...at the renewal of all things, when the Son of Man sits on his glorious throne, you who have followed me will also sit on twelve thrones, judging the twelve tribes of Israel" (Matt.19:28).

When viewed in context, this is an inheritance promise and could be referring to just the twelve or a broader group, based on the words, "you who have followed me." All believers are disciples that follow Jesus. Furthermore, the word "judging" can be taken two ways: as a one-time trial or as one sitting as judge over a long period of time, like all through the millennium. In the latter case, it would be akin to leadership position as king or governor that will lead under the King of kings and Lord of lords and must therefore act in the capacity of judge.

Second, believers will assist Christ at the judgment. The apostle Paul indicates that believers, in general, not just those who are apostles, will participate in the end-time judgment of people and angels (1 Cor.6:1-6).

Third, angels will assist rounding up those to be judged when the Lord returns (Matt.13: 40-42, 49-50).

Fourth, the fact that twelve apostles are used to judge the martyrs raised from the dead at His coming, by extension, they will judge the living as well (Rev.20:4).

We can conclude from both passages that believers will assist our Lord Jesus as judges in the coming Judgment. But we cannot be sure who will specifically judge Israel in addition to the twelve apostles, perhaps Moses, Paul or Billy Graham.

One should bear in mind that the Judgment is the Supreme Court of God Almighty in secession, and from what we have seen from Scripture, there will be several judgment secessions some in heaven, and some on earth. For example, the Believers Judgment will be in heaven (see Volume 2). The judgment of Israel will be on earth, but we cannot say for sure where the final judgment will be (Rev.20:11-15).

For those who think there will only be one judgment session and that is the Final Judgment, should think again. The very fact, we call it the Final Judgment suggest there will be judgments preceding that. If not, why use the word final?

Summary

God has not cast away His covenant people as the apostle Paul so brilliantly argues in Romans, chapters 9 to 11. Despite their unfaithfulness and disobedience to the covenant, God will keep His word. Jesus will return in time to rescue Israel from utter annihilation by the Antichrist's armed forces, He will judge Israel and the Gentiles nations that come against Israel.

Israel will accept Jesus as their Messiah, and they will all be saved that do so. Israel will be allowed to enter the Millennium to witness the Son of David sit on the throne of David and reign over the earth in peace and prosperity as promised.

At last, the Kingdom is restored to Israel. There long looked for Messiah did come to them first as a baby in a manger, and they should have recognized Him because the evidence was overwhelming. The shepherds on a Judean hilltop got the message of the angels, left their flocks, and headed to Bethlehem to worship Him. Strangers from afar came to bend their knees before Him whom heaven and earth adore but Israel's religious leaders stayed home. Even the wicked king Herod for reasons all his own, took the Magi's message seriously and sent out a killing party but Israel's religious leaders stayed home. They had the written revelation of God, how could they!

Israel's lack of faith and their unbelief moved them to reject the Messiah. For that reason, they took this long road of bloody history to bow the knees before Him whom they have so long rejected. How different their history would have been had they not pull down the blinders over their own eyes. Yet, despite such unbelief, God has been faithful and remain true to His covenant. He is indeed the true Covenant Maker and the true Covenant Keeper. Israel, like all of us, has been the covenant braker.

At the return of the Christ, Israel will not be the only nation on earth; there will be many Gentile nations that will survive Armageddon and must face judgment as well. We will look at that next.

CHAPTER 6

THE JUDGMENT OF NATIONS

The *Judgment of the Gentiles* or nations is spoken of vividly in both Old and New Testament Scriptures. In this chapter, we will look at a few key passages that speak to the veracity of this judgment. But we need to bear in mind few important things before we begin this study journey, they will help us to look at things more broadly, and to understand them in context.

First, not all Bible scholars consider the *Judgment of Nations* as a separate judgment from the last or final judgment. In this chapter, the Judgment of Nations is treated as a separate judgment session from the final or last judgment. In fact, the final judgment is dealt with in Volume 9, not this volume.

Second, some scholars see the Judgment of Nations as exclusively based on how nations treated Israel. The position of this book differs; while nations are judged for their treatment of Israel, this judgment is not exclusively for that purpose. There are other matters that will come before this court, that this judgment must dispense with as well. The veracity of this claim will be validated from the Scriptures.

Third, bear in mind as passages from the OT are discussed, that in Bible days nations were spoken of in relation to Israel or as they encountered Israel. That *motif* continued to the early Church, and that mindset still lingers among many Christian scholars and church leaders today.

Fourth, when OT prophets said, God would gather "all nations" at a particular location, and judge them for their treatment of Israel—what does it mean by the word "all?" At the time these prophecies were given, the world was a small place with few nations in existence, and they were not far from each other. Thus, gathering them in one place was, humanly speaking, quite easy. Nations could march to places of war.

The Almighty is all wise and omnipotent but not impractical; gathering the nations of the then known world in one place was not inconceivable and impractical. But the world has changed.

At the writing of this book, there were 195 nations in the world.[1] As of November 2022 according to the UN Report, the world's population is 8 billion.[2] Only China and India have population over a billion. The United States has just under 400 million and Russia under 200 million (i.e., in year 2022).[3]

Fifth, Christianity, at first, did not see itself as a sperate religion from Judaism; the distinction began to be made at the

Council at Jerusalem (Acts 15:1-21). But it still took a while to see itself as a separate institution.[4]

The preceding five things are used as guardrails to our thinking, as we discussed the *Judgment of Nations*. It is God who gives us our intellect, and He does not want us to park it at the church door before we entire. We serve God with our mind, our intellectual faculties. We are commanded to love God with heart, soul, mind, and strength (Deut.6:5; Mark 12:29-31).

The Time of This Judgment

The word "Gentiles" means nations, so in some literature it is referred to as the judgment of the Gentiles or they alternate, while some will just say judgment of the nations. Whichever of these terms is used, it refers to the same group of people.

The Judgment of Nations will take place on earth after the second advent of Christ, after Armageddon, after the judgment of Israel. The place will be Palestine, perhaps Jerusalem.

Since nations will be gathered there for war against Israel, we must assume that one meaning of "all nations" has to do with the major powers, government leaders, massive armies with their support personnel (under the Antichrist of Revelation 13). We would not expect the civilian population of all nations to be there, that is not practical.

The Scriptural Basis

There are many *Old and New Testament Scripture* passages dealing with end-time judgments, some fit the profile for the Judgment of Nations, others do not. We will cite few of the more significant text to make the case for the Judgment of Nations.

First, the prophet Joel indicates that when Israel is restored to their covenant land, God will judge the nations (3:1). The gathering of nations is clear from the following verses:

> I will gather all nations and bring them down to the Valley of Jehoshaphat. There I will put them on trial for what they did to my inheritance, my people Israel, because they scattered my people among the nations and divided up my land. They cast lots for my people and traded boy for wine to drink. (Joel 3:2-3)

The preceding passage gives us time, place, and purpose of this trial or judgment of the nations. **The time** is when Israel is restored to their covenant land. This end-time restoration began with the turn of the 19th century and achieves significance with the modern state of Israel in 1948. The restoration will be completed with the second advent of Jesus Christ.

The place of this trial or judgment is stated—In the Valley of Jehoshaphat in Palestine. The precise location is controversial. There is another location closer to Jerusalem that is associated with the name, Jehoshaphat.[5] In will be in Palestine for sure.

The purpose of the trial is stated—for what they did to my people Israel. ***Who*** **will be on trial?** ***All nations.*** We have already discussed the constraint on the term, "all nations."

The Judgment of Nations appears to be limited to living people only; no resurrection of the dead is spoken of here. That alone disqualifies it from being a general judgment.

Second, the prophet Zechariah (14:1-15) speaks of the war of Armageddon which implies that God will bring the gentile powers against Jerusalem to bring judgment upon them.

War is a form of judgment, throughout history God used war to discipline nations, even His own people Israel. In as much as Zechariah does not speak of a formal trial or judgment, it is greatly implied contextually.

Third, Isaiah (34:1-17) also speaks of Armageddon and the Judgment of Nations but does not spell out a formal trial like Joel; it is contextually implied. Here God addresses all nations, perhaps nations that come against Israel:

> Come near you nations, and listen; pay attention, you people! Let the earth hear, and all that is in it, the world, and all that comes out of it! The Lord is angry with all nations; his wrath is on all their armies. He will totally destroy them, he will give them over to slaughter. Their slain will be thrown out, their dead bodies will stink; the mountains will be soaked with their blood. (Isa.34: 1-3)

Like Zechariah, Isaiah speaks of judgment against the nations with the instrument of war, though no formal trial is indicated.

The flagship New Testament (NT) Scripture for the ***Judgment of Nations*** is Matthew (25: 31-46). It clearly states that:

> When the Son of Man comes in His glory and all the holy angels with Him, then He will sit on the throne of His glory. All the nations will be

gathered before Him, and He will separate them one from another, as a shepherd divides the sheep from the goats. And He will set the sheep on His right hand, but the goats on the left. (Matt.25:31-33 NKJV).

The passage is clear that this is the Judgment of Nations, and that it takes place when Jesus returns to earth. It is also clear that there are two groups of nations, the sheep, and the goats. Jesus is the one that divides them. But on what basis He divides them, and what is the significance?

Note what He the charges are against the sheep nations of which they are not guilty, and for that reason allowed to enter the millennium to reign with Jesus Christ. Here are the charges:

> Then the King will say to those on His right hand, Come, you blessed of my Father, inherit the kingdom prepared for you from the foundation of the word: for I was hungry and you gave Me food; I was thirsty and you gave Me drink, I was a stranger and you took Me in; I was naked and you clothed Me; I was sick and you visited Me, I was in prison and you came to Me.(vv.34-36 NKJV)

The people comprising the sheep nations do not recall ever meeting Jesus personally and rendering those acts of kindness to Him. He said to them, "...inasmuch as you did it to one of the least of these My brethren you did it to Me" (v.40). These people are called righteous based on their relationship with Jesus Christ. Jesus Himself says, "By this shall all men know that you are my disciples, if you have love one for another" (John13:35).

The people that comprise the goat nations have the same charges against them, and they were found guilty. The King said, "inasmuch as you did not do it to one of the least of these, you did not do it to me" (v.45). These are sentence to everlasting punishment for their lack of compassion, love, kindness (v.46).

The passage raises many questions, but the most compelling is, who are those Jesus refers to as *my brethren*? Some scholars say it has to do with Israel for they are blood related to Jesus. That explanation is questionable. Frankly, I do not understand to be limited to Israel on the following basis.

First, Jesus refers to all who do the will of His Father as His brethren. Once, His mother and brothers were concerned about His safety and came to one of His meetings to speak with Him. When it was told to Him that your mother and brothers are outside wanting to speak to Him—He replied, "Who is my mother and who are my brothers? Pointing to his disciples, he said, 'Here are my mother and my brothers. For whoever does the will of my Father in heaven is my brother and sister and mother'" (Matt.12:46-50).

Second, following the example of Jesus, the NT church and the community of faith today refer to each other in family terms: father, mother, sister, brother, elder (Rom.8:12-17;1Tim.5:1-3).

Other Considerations

Huston, we have a problem? Believers in Jesus who are slaughtered toward the end of the tribulation are resurrected as martyrs and judged and given the right of passage to enter and reign with Christ in His millennial kingdom (Rev.20:4-5).

But no judgment is stated for the vast population of earth who are still alive with the mark of the beast and not in the armed forces. This question is not adequately addressed by scholars and worth considering here.

First, according to our Lord Jesus, wide is the gate and broad is the road that leads to destruction, and many enter there on, but small the gate and narrow the road that leads to life and only few find it (Matt.7: 13-14). The implication here is, the numerical loss of souls will be staggering!

If that be the case, of the 8 billion people on earth as of November 2022, more are on the broad road to destruction and will be alive when Jesus returns. Millions of them will have nothing to do with Israel, much more to go to hell for them. This raises issue with the "all nations" term used in connection with the *Judgment of Nations.*

Second, there is no judgment listed for the millions, if not billions of souls, who take the mark of the beast and are still alive in every nation on earth when Jesus returns; they are ordinary civilians not associated with the Antichrist armed forces and are nowhere near Israel during the Armageddon war.

People bearing the mark of the beast will not reign with Christ in the millennial kingdom, so there must be a judgment to dispense of them if they are not included in the Judgment of Nations. Perhaps then, the scope of this judgment is broader than we are willing to admit. But broader how? Let say, just 4 billion are alive with the mark of the beast, will they be all in the region around Israel? That solution is impractical.

Third, perhaps a better way in thinking of the scope of the Judgment of Nation is this--. Since, people of all nations are being judged, chances are they will face judgment in the country where they are, if they have nothing to do with Israel, such as being in the armed forces. The following scenario may apply.

Jesus returns to earth with an army of saints and angels to assist Him in Judgment as Paul and Jesus indicate (Rev.19:11-16; 20:4-5). Will these saints who are given crowns of leadership after the Believers' Judgment conduct judgments concurrently in countries around the world as Christ is presiding in the judgment of nations from Jerusalem? We do not know. But one thing we know, no person bearing the mark of the beast will be allowed to enter the Millennium to reign with Christ; it is for the righteous only (2Tim.2:10-13; Rev.5:10).

Summary

The judgment of nations is a reality, but the Bible does not give us the details, except by implications and inferences. We do not limit God's power do what He says He will do, but we cannot park our intellect, and gloss over issues by invoking God's omnipotence; that is not practical.

The *Judgment of Nations* appears to deal only with living people facing judgment, not resurrected people. The nations gathered in Palestine are undoubtedly ones in the region, and those from elsewhere that hate Israel and travelled to fight against them Israel them in the Armageddon war. They are government leaders, military commanders, and their armies with support personnel, not the civilian population. These nations that gather to annihilate Israel are judged in the Judgment of Nations; that's certain without question.

The scope of this judgment will include the armed forces of nations that come against Israel, but not necessarily limited to them. The judgment of nations is a signal that the Gentile powers have come to an end, in terms of government , military powers or any other control over the earth. But there will be millions, if not billions of civilians who are ordinary citizens of countries all over the world that bear the mark of the beast. These people will not be allowed to enter the millennial reign of Christ and must therefore face judgment.

But nothing is said about these people, so we can only draw inferences from the larger context. Since, Jesus returns to earth with the Church from heaven to reign over the earth, that means, He returns with a government or administration already in place. For example, in the United States, a new administration arrives in Washington D.C. with at least a government in place. Believers are called to heaven at the rapture not just to party, but to be vetted as leaders for a new government. That is one reason for the Believers' Judgment.

The reward of crowns given out in heaven after the believers' judgment are symbols of leadership, as well as the titles of Lords. Jesus returns to earth with many crowns on His head and the titles of KINGS of Kings and LORD of Lords; all this signal that He does not return to rule alone (Rev.19:11-16).

The seat of His government will be in Jerusalem, that is where throne David was and will be. Jesus will sit on the throne of David as the KING of Kings and LORD of Lords (Isa.9:6-7). This suggest there will be Kings and Lords in His administration throughout the word that Jesus would be ruling over. Like an archangel is an angel that rules over other angels, and an archbishop rules over other bishops, so the KING of Kings rules over kings and lord, and various other titles of leadership.

This further suggest that the judgment of nations is, perhaps worldwide in scope, with the apostles on thrones judging the twelve tribes of Israel, and others sitting on thrones ruling and judging in other parts of the world. This would explain "the all nations before Him" scenario.

Furthermore, it would explain the expression, *my brethren*, giving the broader applicability beyond Jesus' immediate brothers and sisters to a larger followship. Jesus used the term to refer to all His followers that do the will of His Father.

How we treat people, our neighbors, our fellow human beings, especially those who are in need, and those in the righteous community are of great spiritual significance to the administration of heaven and earth.

From the Judgment of Nations and other Scripture passages, we can also conclude that several nations will enter the millennial reign with Christ. But we must also admit that we do not know all the details and we are in no position to be dogmatic. By all measures, the people of God have a bright future and have every reason to rejoice and live in hope.

ARMAGEDDON

CHAPTER 7

THE SALVATION OF ISRAEL

The salvation of humankind is no small matter to God; He has invested the life of His Son to make it a reality. God is love and salvation is rooted in the heart of that love (John 3:16; 1 John 4:7-10). God has been occupied with salvation from the very beginning of time. Revelation (3:8) informs us that Jesus is "the Lamb who was slain from the creation of the world."

God demonstrated the need for salvation to the human family shortly after the Fall of man in the Paradise Garden. God took the life an animal as a substitute for the lives of Adam and Eve. The blood served as temporary cover for their sins, and the skin covered their nakedness (Gen.3:21). But that was a short-term solution to a long-term problem. God speaks of a permanent solution with the perfect sacrifice to come (Gen.3:

15). The sacrifice of Abel was type of the permanent atonement to come. This blood atonement is also reflected in the sacrifices of the Levitical system to come later under Moses' leadership.

In his epistle to the Galatians, Paul gives us this intelligence report, "But when the set time was fully come, God sent his Son, born of a woman, born under the law, to redeem those under the law, that we might receive adoption of sonship" (Gal.4:4-5). Paul was referring to the person whom John the Baptist identified for Israel when he said, "Behold the Lamb of God who takes away the sin of the world!" (John 1:29, 36).

God's plan of salvation emerged from eternity into time, not suddenly or at once, but as an unfolding drama over time to full revelation in Jesus Christ, the Son of God.

A Unified Way of Salvation

Humankind is diverse in terms of race, culture, and nationality, but God has only one plan of salvation for all people, be they Jews or Gentiles. That plan is through a person, and that person was first revealed by name by the angel Gabriel to the blessed Virgin Mary as Yeshua (Matt.1:18-21; Luke 1:16-38).

God has one sacrifice for sin, and that sacrifice is the person of Jesus Christ, the Lamb of God (John 1: 29-35). The epistle to the Hebrews emphasizes Christ as the one sacrifice, offered once unto God for the salvation of all people (Heb.9:26, 10:12). Jesus Christ is the One access to God for all humankind (John 14:6; Rom.5:1-5). The Bible provides no alternative path!

There is the tendency for some people to think Jews have an advantage with God; they can bypass Jesus Christ. But the apostle Paul put that false concept to rest (Rom.3:9). The Jew has no advantage over the Gentile when it comes to salvation from sin; they all are sinners and must come to God through Jesus Christ by faith (3:20, 5:1-2). If one group has advantage over the other, then God would have two or more standard of righteousness for humankind to measure up to. But there is one standard, and that is Jesus Christ Himself.

Let me emphasize, God does not offer multiple ways of salvation, and the Bible, God's Word does not teach multiple ways of salvation. The Bible teaches that "Salvation is found in no one else, for there is no other name under heaven given to mankind by which me must be saved" (Acts 4:12).

The name Yeshua (Jesus), though a common name in first century Israel, was not made known as the name the Redeemer would take until it was disclosed to the blessed Virgin Mary by Gabriel. But certain unique characteristics were revealed hundreds of years before Yeshua arrived, so Israel could easily identify Him. Let's look at few of these unique identifiers.

Messiah's Identifying Characteristics

Satan (using the serpent) was the personality who deceived the woman and her husband in the Paradise Garden to disobey God's command. That act of defiance, violated the sovereign, executive order of God, and released the curse of death on Adam and Eve and their posterity (Gen.1:16-17,3:1-24).

Immediately after the Fall, God made this declaration and promise, "I will put enmity between you and the woman, and between your offspring and hers; he will crush your head, and you will strike his heel" (Gen.3:15). This is the first identification (ID) of the Redeemer to come. He would be the "seed of the woman" instead of the seed of the man. Theologians refer to the announcement of this good news as the "*proto-euaggelion.*"

The call of Abraham and the covenant made with him identified a people through whom the Redeemer/Messiah would come to bless all the families of the earth (Gen.12:1-3,15:1-21,17:1-27). God continued to clarity the Messianic lineage as Isaac, Jacob, Judah, a prophet like Moses, a Son of David, to be born of a Virgin, in Bethlehem of Judea (Isa.7:14; Micah 5:2).

The Messiah would be both human and divine in nature as evidence by His names: "Immanuel" (God with us), "Wonderful Counselor, the Mighty God, the Everlasting Father, Prince of Peace" (Isa. 7:14-15, 9:6-7).

The Messiah will be a King from the royal lineage of David and will sit upon his throne, and rule over a kingdom that is everlasting; the responsibility of government will be upon His shoulders. His will be a kingdom one of peace, righteousness, and justice with no end (Isa.9:7).

The Messiah would be a suffering servant, a substitutionary sacrifice for the redemption of His people, Israel (Isa.53).The Messiah will be the deliverer and Savior of His people Israel (Matt.1:18-21). The angel Gabriel's message to the Virgin Mary made it clear how the child is conceived, whose Son He is, what His name is, and what His mission would be (Luke 1:26-38).

The mother of the Messiah was confirmed Elizabeth by divine revelation. As Mary entered her presence, baby John the Baptist in Elizabeth's womb leaped for joy and Elizabeth was filled with the Holy spirit. She suddenly exclaimed, "Blessed are you among women and blessed is the child you will bear! But why am I so favored, that the mother of my Lord should come to me?" (vv.39-45).

Mary's testimony concerning the Christ child she was bearing further confirms the Messiah to Israel. She worshiped and prophesied saying, "My soul magnifies the Lord, and my spirit has rejoiced in God my Savior; for He has regarded the lowly stat of maidservant; for behold, from henceforth all generations will call me blessed. For He who is mighty has done great things for me, and holy is His name..." (vv.46-49 NKJV).

There is the revelation to Joseph, convincing him to change his mind from quietly divorcing Mary to going ahead and marry Mary instead (Matt.1:19-21).

The revelations of the Messiah to Israel are too numerous to condense in one chapter of a small book such as this. There is the census being declared by Caesar Augustus that brought Joseph and Mary to Bethlehem of Judea, not knowing that their child would be born there in fulfillment of prophecy (Luke 2:1-7). There is the announcement by angels to the shepherd on the Judean Hillside (vv.8-20).

There is the pilgrimage of the Magi who traveled long and far in search of the Christ child (Matt.2:1-2). There is the madness of king Herod to kill the child (vv.3-18).

The list of revelations about the Messiah, signs, prophecies continue to his death, resurrection, and beyond. How could His people Israel that have custody of the Word of God be so blind that they missed their own Messiah. This could be nothing but willful ignorance.

Salvation and Sacrifice

From the Fall of man in the Paradise Garden, salvation was promise (Gen.3:15). That salvation involves blood sacrifice (3:21, 4:1-9). Why blood? The answer is simple yet propound; it is because of the nature of sin.

Sin is a capital crime against God and His Kingdom; the penalty is death (Gen.3:15-7; Rom.6:23). Adam, the father of the human race sinned, and since all human beings were in Adam, we all sinned and died with him (Rom.5:12; 1Cor.15:21).

Animal life as well as human life is in the blood. Humans are created in God's image; they are above the brute, beast creation but a little lower than the angelic creation (Heb.2:5-8). Animals are a lesser life form of life; their lives cannot take the place of human life, nor their blood atone for sins of humans in any way (Heb.9 13--15). For that reason God provides Himself a special sacrifice for the redemption or salvation of the human family in the person of His Son, Jesus Christ (John 3:13-17).

God accepted the blood of animal sacrifice as a temporary cover for sin until the perfect sacrifice, the Lamb of God, in the person of the Messiah, Jesus Christ arrives (John 1:29-35). The Messiah is the seed of the woman, the Son of God, so he is sinless. For that reason, His precious blood would atone for the sins of all humans (3:16).

The entire sacrificial system of the Old Testament was intended to be temporary; it points to Christ the perfect and permanent sacrifice. Those who by faith trust God under that system were looking forward to the cross, while we on this side of the cross who by faith trust God for our salvation are looking back at the cross. Abraham, Isaac, Jacob, Moses and all the others are redeemed by the blood of Jesus that was shed on the cross. Apart from Christ and His cross, there is no redemption or salvation; it is the only system God has to save both Jews and Gentiles.

The Rejection of Jesus

A person, Jesus Christ had to come through a woman, that woman had to be part of a family, that family part of a tribe, that tribe part of a nation; that's the way the world was organized then. That woman turned out to be the blessed Virgin Mary, the family belong to the lineage of David, the tribe Judah, the nation Israel, God's covenant people. The people with the Word of God: The Torah, the Prophets, and the Writings.

When Jesus finally showed up, He offered salvation to Israel first, but the leaders of Israel said, no, you are not the Messiah we were looking for (John 1:12). They rejected Him and had Him crucified (John 18-19).

But, in as much as the leaders of Israel rejected the Messiah, many of the common people received Him gladly, even those who became His disciples. The early church started out with Jews and gradually transition to be predominantly Gentiles.

Israel is still waiting for the Messiah to come. Since, AD 70 when the Romans destroyed Jerusalem, Israel is without a temple, without sacrifice, and without salvation from sin. They have invented a worship system without sacrifice, without a savior and salvation. Such things cannot be found outside of Jesus Christ. Their unbelief disqualifies them from being saved.

But does that mean God has cast away His covenant people? No! But they have cast God away by breaching the covenant. Abraham's part of the covenant is unconditional (Gen.12:1-5;

15:1-21;17:1-27). Abraham and his descendants through Isaac would hold the "title deed to the land of Palestine."[1] Israel would continue as a nation to possess the land, and she will be redeemed so she can enjoy the blessings forever and bless the nations of the world. God bound Himself to it and will bring to pass what is stated in the covenant.[2] But the covenant does not end with Abraham; it continued with Moses.

The Mosaic part of the covenant is conditional; it has to do with inheriting the land, staying on the land, prospering on the land, being the head nation among nations, not the tail. This part of the covenant has terms of faith and obedience attached for Israel to keep; see the terms here (Deut.28:1-68). If Israel forsakes Yahweh to serve other gods, that is considered a breach of the covenant, and would result in them been driven off the land and scattered among the nations, to the ends of the earth. But God would regather them from among those nations in the latter days, and bring them back to their covenant land, and they will never be uprooted again. That restoration is underway since the turn of the late 19th century. But the covenant does not end with Moses; it continues with David.

The Davidic part of the covenant is that someone from David's lineage will always sit on David's throne and rule over his kingdom forever and all the nations of the world will be blessed through Him (Ps. 89:3-4,34-36; Isa.9:6-7; Jer.23:5-6).

Undoubtedly, this person spoken of by the prophets in the Hebrew Bible is Israel's Messiah, Jesus Christ. When He returns the forever part of the covenant will be realized. Israel will go through a transformation or rebirth on two level: natural and spiritual. The natural rebirth of Israel is significantly underway with the modern State of Israel, the spiritual rebirth will take place when Yeshua returns, and they embrace Him as their Messiah. Any Jew or Gentile who holds out against that reality is permanently lost. There is no other sacrifice or path to eternal life.

All Israel will Be Saved

Salvation was offered first to the Jews, not because they had preferred treatment with God, but because they were the instrument chosen to bring the Messiah and salvation to the world of humankind. But their unbelief disqualifies them from such mission; the task was given to the Church. But the Church does not replace Israel (John 1:12; Matt.28:19-20).

Israel's unfaithfulness does not cancel out this tripartite covenant God made with them. They will be restored to the land and in the end, all Israel will be saved (Rom.11 25-27). But what is meant by all Israel?

It does not mean that unbelieving Jews who stubbornly refused to embrace Yeshua as their Messiah will be saved despite their unbelief, no it does not mean that. God does not have two plans of salvation: one for Jews and one for Gentiles.

God is preserving a Jewish remnant for Himself, and He will prepare them to receive their Messiah, Jesus Christ. So, some Jews have come, and are coming to faith in Jesus Christ during the Church age, that is from Pentecost to the Rapture (Acts 214-47; 1Thess.4:16). We call them messianic Jews today.

During the Great Tribulation special efforts will be made to evangelized Israel through the ministry of the 144,000 Jewish evangelist. It is evident that God is focusing His attention again on the Jews during this time. The blindness will have fallen from their eyes, and millions will come to salvation through Yeshua. Others will be softened and ready to embrace Jesus when He is revealed to Israel at His second advent.

But even so millions will be lost before Yeshua shows up in person to rescue the nation of Israel from hostile, genocidal gentile powers. Unbelief has consequences whether you are Jewish or Gentile. Billions of gentiles will also be lost.

Israel will play a significant role in the Millennial rule of the Christ. He will rule from Jerusalem. Israel will also play a significant role in the eternal City of God because each of the twelve gates to the city has one of the tribes of Israel, and the names of the apostles (also Jewish) will be on the twelve foundations of the city. God is faithful and keeps His word!

Conclusion

The Great Tribulation will serve as a purifying instrument for Israel; it will prepare Israel psychologically and spiritually to receive the true Messiah, Jesus Christ. Millions of Jews and Gentiles too will come to Jesus Christ. But the focus is Israel.

The Great Tribulation is the final fire of suffering for Israel; the antichrist will heat the oven of annihilation a hundred times hotter to permanently silence the Jews and their so-called covenant. But many have sought to silence them before: the Egyptians, Assyrians, the Babylonians, the Persians, the Romans, the Germans, and many other devils in between. They all have tried extinguishing the Jewish flame and failed; Jews remain a resilient people, always rising from the ashes to bloom again.

From AD 70 to Hitler's Germany, the Gentile world turned up the heat on the Jews, but the fire could not destroy them. God would not allow it. So, Satan went back to the drawing board and has come up with a bold plan of annihilation. Now He has the necessary firepower to do what others could not do, full annihilation of the Jewish State and her people. And it has gotten the God Abraham angry, and His fury has waxed hot (Isa. 63: 1-6). The result is Armageddon. Israel's Messiah will destroy the collective Gentile powers that come against Israel.

Israel will suffer great losses during the Armageddon military campaign, but not enough to destroy the Jewish State and its people, because God would not allow it. Those that that lose their physical lives by standing against worshipping the antichrist will rise again to enter the millennial reign with Christ, because they are martyrs (Rev.20:4).

Armageddon is more than the war that ends all wars. It is God rescuing His covenant people from annihilation and bringing judgment and justice upon the Gentiles. The rescue of Israel will further open Israel's eyes that Yeshua is indeed the Messiah, resolving any lingering doubts or pockets of unbelief.

ARMAGEDDON

END NOTES

Chapter 1

1. Merrill F. Unger, *The New Unger's Bible Dictionary*. Edited by R.K. Harrison. Chicago, IL: Moody Bible Institute, Revised 1988, 103.
2. Ibid.
3. Ibid.
4. A.W. Pink, *The Sovereignty of God*. New Kensington, PA: Whitaker House, 2016, 25-36.

Chapter 2

1. Nobel Prize: https://www.nobelprize.org/prizes/lists/all-nobel-prizes/ (access 11/19/2022).
2. https://en.wikipedia.org/wiki/List_of_Jewish_Nobel_laureates (access 11/29/2022).
3. Rabbi Kirt A. Schneider, *The Lion of Judah.* Lake Mary, FL: Charisma House Book Group, 2015, 95-96.
4. *Ibid.*
5. Benjamin Netanyahu. *A Durable Peace, Israel and Its Place among the Nations.* New York: Grand Central Publishing, 1993, 10

6. https://en.wikipedia.org/wiki/Balfour_Declaration
7. Theodor Herzl, *A Jewish State. First published in English in London 1896, translated by Sylvie d' Avigdor. Now and Then Reader edition 2016.*
8. Benjamin Netanyahu, *A Durable Peace, Israel and Its Place Among the Nations.* New York: Grand Central Publishing, 1993, 10.
9. https://en.wikipedia.org/wiki/Balfour_Declaration
10. A Durable Peace, 10.
11. *Ibid.*
12. *Holman Study Bible*, NKV. Nashville, TN: Holman Bible Publishers, 2015, 2168.

Chapter 3
1. J. Dwight Pentecost. *Things T. Come, A Study in Biblical Eschatology.* Grand Rapids, MI: Zondervan, 1958, 416.
2. Benjamin Netanyahu. *A Durable Peace*, 55-57.
3. https://www.jewishvirturallibrary.org/text-of-the-balfour-declaration (accessed 12/21/2022).
4. A Durable Peace, 56-58.

Chapter 4
1. The New Unger's Bible Dictionary, 259.
2. Ibid, 259.
3. Ibid, 605

Chapter 6
1. https://www.worldometers.info/geography/how-many-countries-are-there-in-the-world
2. https://worldpopulationreview.com/
3. Ibid.

4. *The Lion of Judah*, 23-39
7. J. Dwight Pentecost. *Things T. Come, A Study in Biblical Eschatology*. Grand Rapids, MI: Zondervan, 1958, 416.

Chapter 7

1. J. Dwight Pentecost. *Things to Come*, 72-73
2. *Ibid.*
3. *Ibid.*

ARMAGEDDON

ABOUT THE AUTHOR

Michael W. Dewar, Sr. is a pastor, Bible teacher, a mentor in the spiritual life, a Licensed Master Social Worker, and a specialist in conflict management and resolution. He trains Agents of Peace-Managers of Conflicts to launch peace ministries in local churches.

Reverend Dewar is the founder and pastor of New York Congregational Baptist Church (NYCBC), and the author of several books, including a three-volume training course on *Church and Family Conflicts.*

He holds earned degrees from several institutions of higher learning, including the Master of Divinity from what is now Palmer Theological Seminary, Eastern University, the MSW from Wurzweiler School of Social Work, Yeshiva University, the LMSW from the State of New York, and the D.MIN. from Regent University, School of Divinity.

Rev. Dewar lives in NYC with his family.

Fight the good fight of faith, lay hold on eternal life.

OTHER BOOKS BY THIS AUTHOR

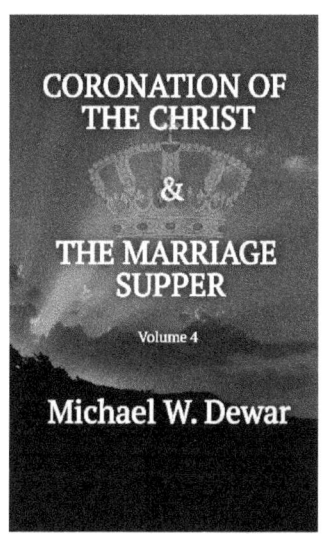

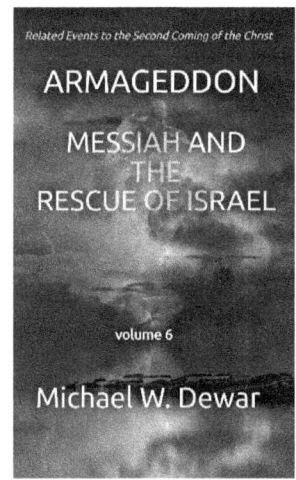

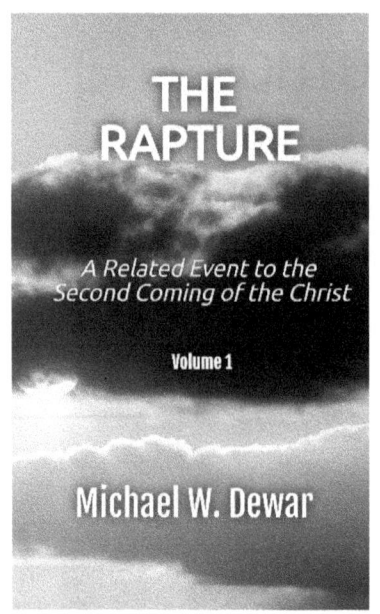

Volume 3

OTHER BOOKS BY THIS AUTHOR

Conflict Resolution Course
For Churches
******

Start a peace ministry in your church.

Textbook

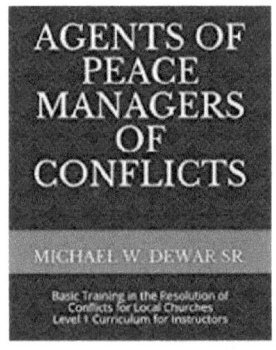

Instructor's Manual

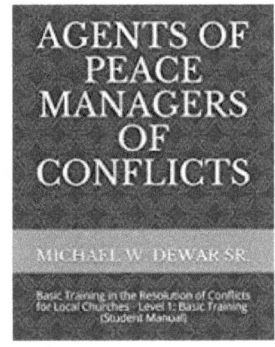

Students' Manual

OTHER BOOKS BY THIS AUTHOR

Have you ever had your dwelling place spiritual cleansed? Spiritual desecration is worst that natural dirt in your house; get the mess cleaned up and live better longer. Begin with this eye-opening book.

FEEDBACK

Visit DSPCleansing.com and join our mailing list.

ARMAGEDDON

www.ingramcontent.com/pod-product-compliance
Lightning Source LLC
Chambersburg PA
CBHW071716040426
42446CB00011B/2087